Ever
Is New Again

30 Years of
Writers on the Avenue

Muscatine, Iowa

Dedicated
to all those who have supported WOTA
throughout the years

WRITERS ON THE AVENUE

CONTENTS

Premier Edition

Muscatine, Iowa

Writers on the Avenue

A collection of stories, poems and essays from members and friends of Writers on the Avenue.

Summer 1991

EDITOR'S NOTE

In late 1989, Duffy De France, Sally Stiles, and Wendi Lee saw the need for a writer's support group in Muscatine where people could meet to talk writing and share work. They were active in the local chapter of the American Pen Women, but they wanted a group that could include men. The new group first met in February 1990. Sally Stiles coined the name Writers on the Avenue, and it stuck. (But see Dan Moore's imagined origin story on page 111.)

Artists in Action gave the group a home and WOTA began meeting the last Tuesday of each month at 7:00 pm. There were no dues and no agenda. Writers brought in a short story, poems, or essays for critique. From the beginning, the goal was to establish a supportive atmosphere where writers could offer constructive feedback and learn to improve their craft.

In 1991, Writers on the Avenue published its first anthology through the combined efforts of Wendi Lee, Rick Noel, Karen Sternberg, and Duffy De France. It featured the work of Quad Cities writers David R. Collins, Kit Redeker, and Dick Stahl as well as Muscatine writers who would go on to become WOTA stalwarts, among them Aldeen Davis, Kitty Jones, Nadine Lord, Lucile Adkins Eye, and Dan Titus. Some were accomplished, multi-published authors; some were beginners; all were welcome.

As the composition of the group changed, so did its structure. WOTA established a mission as a nonprofit literary arts organization with a board of officers, a treasury, and bylaws. Dues were originally $5 a year.

Over the years, WOTA met at bookstores, Muscatine Community College, and Musser Public Library. WOTA members were frequently active in the community arts scene, participating in annual Muscatine events like the Holiday Stroll and partnering with other literary groups like the Shadow Writers club, the Riverbend Storytellers, and the Society of Great River Poets, with whom WOTA has sponsored creativity retreats since 1998. WOTA has also held occasional literary contests to inspire local writers, and they've always been welcoming to and encouraging of youth.

In addition to anthologies published when funds and time afforded, WOTA members like to tackle collaborative storytelling projects. One example, a round-robin book named *Highway 61*, has been years in the making. For a while WOTA member Tina Boldt published a monthly newsletter that featured WOTA news, pieces from members, and writing inspiration. At some point, dues went up to $10 a year.

While WOTA is open to all sorts of writing as long as it's suitable for general audiences, an ongoing tradition at meetings is to decide on a writing prompt to inspire work for the next month. A long-running favorite is the WOTA Word Challenge. Each writer at the meeting contributes a word and the challenge is to generate a piece of writing using all the words on the list. Results are extremely varied and often hilarious, as samples in the following pages will demonstrate.

In 2016 WOTA incorporated into an Iowa literary nonprofit, which means it still has a board and bylaws but is now tax-exempt. There's a website and a monthly newsletter, now electronic. In recent years WOTA has held two poetry contests and a poetry festival, run book tables at Muscatine events including Second Saturday, hosted writing workshops, funded scholarships for Creativity Retreats, and published four anthologies featuring WOTA members along with other established and emerging writers. The group meets twice a month at Musser Public Library, and dues are still $10. The mission holds true: WOTA aims to create a supportive environment where writers of all ages, styles, genres, and levels of experience can share work, get feedback, and improve their craft.

The following anthology captures the many voices that have contributed to WOTA over the last 30 years: founders who got the whole enterprise going and helped steer the ship; long-standing members who have pushed the group forward, some who served for years, some who left and came back; and the recent additions who have given the group new life. We're delighted to share this celebratory volume with you and we look forward to serving area writers and the literary arts for many more years to come.

For information on meetings and events, visit our website at http://writersontheavenue.wordpress.com or email wotamuscatine@gmail.com. New members are always welcome.

Misty Urban, past president and editor-in-chief
Muscatine, March 2020

PART ONE

ECHOES

Duffy De France

IN PURSUIT OF PERFECTION

A trail of pig grass, I crush it, walk into clear
    summer air to an abandoned farmhouse
Once we lived there, the land of baked clay
    too many rocks, withering summers
    scorched our crops, our souls. Still, you can
see our small handprints in the cracked cement
    scribbled words we wrote – Endeavor, Perfect,
    Beauty, Utopia, Persistence, Learn, Future.
What was Dad thinking? The owner spoiled the soil
    Dad rotated crops, poured manure, composted
    shaping healthy crops to grow again.
Suddenly, sold! We moved twice more to doctor
    the land, perfect for Iowa crops, 4-H, farm life.
We gave up during the farm crisis, let the weeds
    cover the tall grass, handprints, cement words

WEEDS

We were weeds growing up
clothes exaggerated
manners sparse
We embarrassed the lilies and roses,
blowing milk weed pods
and dandelion seeds all over
their nice green lawns
AND SPIT ON THEIR TULIPS.

NOTHING GROWS ON PEBBLES

The Emperor is crowned in diamonds
    The people in pebbles and beads
The Empress is garbed in velvet and satin
    The people clothed in rags
The Emperor sits on a golden throne
    The people have no chairs
The Palace is scented with perfumes
    The huts reek of slum living
The Empress has but one child
    The women have too many
The Royal Tables are supplied abundantly
    The people beg for food
The Empire rests on shifting sands
    The people wait for winds to blow it away.

FINAL SOCCER GAME

In the burn of July, we seek
    the awning of green
    to set our thin blanket
        painting a scene with
        basket of melon
    and your dad's too-strong wine

Our lips pattern
        the only glass
        watching
    my nephew's championship match

Passing the paper cup
    as often as the ball
        from goal to goal

with your words/my words
        sinking, stooping
        cascading, bantering
    between two opposing forces
    never quite going out-of-bounds

Before the referee's final whistle
        you crush the chalice
        and make a penalty kick
    I walk off the field

DRIFTING

Drifting down the Mississipp'
Into which my paddle slips
I watch a seagull take a dip
As I drift slowly on.

Floating past the muddy bank
And wooded shores so dark and dank
I pass a derelict that sank
As I drift slowly on.

I scan the stream from shore to shore
Upstream and down till eyes are sore
And note the flotsam more and more
As I drift slowly on.

Assorted junk floats here and there
An oil drum, a broken chair
I wonder, don't the people care?
As I drift slowly on.

I'm saddened, and I harbor fears
That in a few more fleeting years
The dear old stream will flow with tears
As we drift slowly on.

I long to see before I die
The river, 'neath the clear blue sky
Clean and pleasing to my eye
As I drift slowly on.

PIE AND COFFEE

I walked into a small café a week or so ago
To get a cup of coffee and pie à la mode
But I discovered on that day
From the chair on which I sat
That the waitress couldn't bring me just pie and coffee
No, it wasn't as simple as that.

"What kind of apple pie?" she asked.
"What kind indeed," says I to her,
"I want the kind that's made from apples."
She said, "I know that, sir,
But we have apples of different kind,
If I know what pleases you best,
We'll make your pie from that alone
And forget about all the rest."

"We have Yellow Delicious and Red Delicious
And a type that's a little of each,
We have Crab Apples, Jonathans, and bright red Romes
And one that tastes more like a peach.
We have domestic apples and foreign apples
And some that taste better in jam.
We have summer apples and winter apples
And some we get straight from the can."

"Well, I really don't know," says I to her,
"So I'll tell you what I think it should be.
I think the Jonathon type, my dear
Would be the most pleasing to me."

"Very well," she said to me,
And wrote something down on a pad,
"The kind of apples we have straightened out,
Now what kind of pie will you have?"

"We have apple cobblers that taste really great,
We have French apple and Dutch apple too.
We have crumb apple pie and fresh apple dumpling
Or a great apple strudel for you.
We have strawberry/apple and apple/rhubarb,
What more could your tummy desire?"
I thought and I thought and I thought on it more,
Until I thought my brain would expire.

So I ordered a cup of coffee
While I battled this problem some more.
"What kind of coffee would you like today, sir?"
Hadn't we been through this bit once before?
So I said to this lass with my brightest of smiles,
To keep my brain from going over the border,
"Just bring me the pie and the coffee, my dear,
That you'd pick if you were to order."

"The Hill of Life" by Dan Titus
Inscribed on the Greenwood Cemetery steps
Muscatine, IA

Katherine E. Jones

SOMEDAY WHEN OLD

Someday when old I'll be as free
As thistledown and errant bee
A whole September afternoon
Interpreting a cricket's tune
And watching the bronzing of the trees.
The winter birds will be my guests
When seems the world has gone to rest
December dusks will early come
A quiet snow will early fall
When I am old.

From cottage deck on nights in June
I'll watch the river shadow strewn
From mornings gold to evenings dark
Then see the early stars come out
Unhurried now I'll wait to see
Slope softly to eternity
When I am old someday.

WHEN I AM OLD

When I am old (I am eighty)
I am not going to wear lavender
Or a lace collar,
Or sit in a rocking chair
With a shawl around my shoulders.
I am not going to holler, "Huh?
Stop mumbling, talk!"
When I can't hear.
No, I am going shopping.
I am going to buy a bright red hat,
A pair of red high-heeled shoes,
And if I wobble when I walk,
I shall carry a cane.
Not an ordinary cane but one with a gold handle.
I am going to spend my children's inheritance
And live life to its fullest,
Then maybe just maybe I won't have time to die.

SUNSET

In a glorious wave
    of yellow and red,
"Good night," the King
    has silently said,
And marched around
    earth's corner to bed.

HUMILITY

I grow an inch
    and want applause
And all the while
    the rose —

Bud and blooms
    in my backyard
And only God
    gives pause.

Aldeen Davis

THE EBONY MOTH

The ebony moth, beautiful,
    drawn to the candle's light
    bright, flaming candle light
Slowly, for half a century,
    good deeds, works faithfully applied
Striving to perfect, with tears,
    laughter, she draws
    closer to the flame.

Leaping higher, brighter, stronger
    the flame flickers, welcoming
    the sacrifice soon to be made.
Now weary, worn, the ebony moth
    is drawn
    closer to the altar of time.
With folded wings, supplication,
    the moth enters the light
The candle, now
    brighter than before.

PIPE DREAM

I watch my son, the boy,
Eyes bright with anticipation,
Blow crystalline, perfect bubbles
From a pipe: Fireman,
Doctor, Astronaut, President

I watch my son, the man,
No longer innocent but
A dreamer still,
The sweet acrid puffs from the pipe
Float upward
Eyes dimmed by the false charms
Of that temptress.

Tomorrow they will come:
My friends,
Mary Ann, Rock, Harri, Angel,
They will bring the dream.

 I watch my son.
Gone is the pipe as
Six strong men carry him
To his final resting place
To lie for eternity
With his dreams.

Tomma Lou Maas

EARTH METALS

He strung blue lapis
around my neck for love
and Chinese turquoise
long life beads
for cancer

he poured garnets
in my hand
like wine flowing from a chalice
when I could not eat
and draped long strands of pearls
around my throat when I grew old

he brought me amber from the Baltic Sea
and malachite from Moldova,
he hunted tiger's eyes far south
in Africa

he found two dolphins kissing —
silver hearts molded for Valentine's Day —
and slipped them in my ears

he captured a dragonfly
immortal in silver and gold,
he found a crab made of jasper
in Madagascar, warrior to my cancer

he gave me lucky jades
of many colors and
brought moonstones from Ceylon

he laid agates in my hand
-picked from the Little Cedar
where he fishes and told
me stories of the bass
and how he let her go.

Nadine Lord

THE QUEST OF EMILY DICKINSON

Poetically ambitious
    intellectually elite—
Fiercely independent
    privately discreet—
Culturally enriched
    emotionally deprived—
Religiously ambivalent
    but her poet's soul survived.

Mike Fladlien

AFTER SCHOOL RIPPLES

Sometimes I feel
like a drop of water
falling from a leaf
into a lake
making ripples
that at first
make a difference
then disappear.

Betty Mowery

THE DANCER

Sometimes, when white pills dull
	arthritic pain, and locked doors
	and drawn shades shut out a lonely
	night, she slips on ballet slippers.
She carefully ties frayed laces,
	glances at the yellowed poster
	proclaiming opening night, then
	toward a dust covered piano
	in the corner.
Her cluttered apartment, with its
	sparse food stamp supplies,
	is the stage; a bare bulb
	hanging from a fly-specked
	cord, the spotlight.
As memory music plays in her mind,
	her brown spotted hands raise
	gracefully, an imagined pirouette.
Her pretended, graceful movements
	return the feeling of being one
	with the dance, the music.
For a moment, she is young,
	strong, and happy.

But soon the freedom of movement
    slips away, and pain creeps back
    into her tired body.
The cat meows to be fed, and the
    couple next door yell angrily
    at each other,
    as she slips off the ballet slippers.

Kit Redeker

THE TOWERS

All that is left of the great woods
they call the Limberlost
runs along a crooked creek
in eastern Indiana.
I saw the sun set into it once
on a long summer day
when we drove to see Geneva Porter's
log cabin that used to sit
at its edge. Millions of acres it
was, prime oak and pine, rich from
swampy brown soil.

I closed my eyes against the sunset
and remembered the men who corded
roads through, whose axes felled
one great tree after another.
They wore leather leggings against
the silent swamp snakes; lumberbosses rode
wide-backed horses, wore high black
boots. Trees crashed on forest floor
by the millions to build Chicago...
and then the Limberlost went up
in the smoke of the Great Fire.

Sometimes, when I'm shopping at Watertower,
I think of Gene Stratton Porter
photographing butterflies or
spinning her tale of Freckles and
the Swamp Angel.

Funny how the skyscrapers
aren't so tall beside the memory
of that great forest

RED PAINT SALE

Dad never told me why he smashed
his old smokehouse bricks into powder
so fine I couldn't stop spitting
dragon's fire in the hay barn.

He never explained buttermilk souring
in the sun for days or the black clouds
of flies storming his rings of open cans.

He never wiped his whiskered face
when his dehorned cattle sprayed blood
like a thumb-pressed hose
into wide lipped jugs
or cleaned his apron, its red islands
stained like a dancing butcher's.

In his shed, he mixed paint
like shiners mix whiskey. On hot nights,
he stirred his cauldrons
with a ladle, popping
red boils like some spector spanking
off-key sopranos
in the Devil's chorus.

After harvest, he painted the cow barn
so high a gloss the neighbor's bulls
stampeded his fence lines
like juggernauts
to sink their horns
into something solid red.

Dad said all this was good for business.
He sold the paint in ten gallon cans,
freeing the stuck beasts
only after their owners smiled
like poker raisers
when paying every price hike.

Mary Kay Lane

HOT SKATIN' BARBIE VISITS THE NATIVITY

An Infant, an inch and a half long, sleeps
on glass hay while white porcelain kings
bear gifts to his impoverished parents.
A star shines over the crystal crèche
And the animals are silent as stones.
All is peaceful
in the stable on my coffee table.
But into the tranquility comes a turbulence:
Hot Skatin' Barbie
rollerblades in, her hot pink helmet askew,
her blonde hair billowing,
her cleavage conspicuous.
I wonder, oh God,
what can she have for the Lord?
Then the glitter from her Spandex bodysuit
falls on baby Jesus and I think,
He does look good in glitter.
It makes him glow.

Patricia Regan Argiro

ADVISEMENT

Take words. Seriously. But take
care that such seriously taken
words do not turn, glancing like
scimitars that, cared too much for,
can kill you with your own hand.

Take rhythm, rhyme. Act verbs.
Count syllables as they, dancing,
move across your mind, spilling
onto your tongue and falling
outside you into the earless air.

Care carefully, maintaining
mundane concerns for food and
drink: clean rooms, fed cats.
Protect your sanity.
Still, above all, take words'
arrangement seriously.
But not so seriously as to
exclude the living word.

THE MARRIAGE QUILT

Woven, as bells toll,
    with threads both strong and
    weak
Fibers that pull and strain
    as years go by
Threads that snap to expose holes,
    empty and widening
Colors that fade and pale
    with the passing years

Reinforce the strained threads
    with stronger
Replace the faded colors
    with bright
Mend the holes with patches
    of good memories
Embroider the edges with
    sturdy red hearts,
        forgiving and laden with love.

"They're post-it notes. I dreamed up all sorts
of ideas for my next next book."

Daniel Roberts

Sharon Savage

DISPATCHES FROM DOWNTOWN

On all hollow's eve when you're fast asleep
and spiders go marching down old Second Street
    climb up out of the sewers
        join with the rats
gather all creatures to elect the stray cats
or the toads for dominion of all that they meet
while creeping and crawling down old Second Street

As they climb up the lamp posts and take the main stage
the cats meow loudly in anger and rage
    and have the advantage
        'cause toads only croak
and aren't nearly as loud as the other foul folk,
are pudgy and warty with webbed little feet
that wobble them bobbly down old Second Street

So they make up tall tales about histories and votes
and dig up all stupid and crazy old quotes
    that make them look bad
        and unfit for the job
and incite all the creatures to one monstrous mob
who think studying the issues should be obsolete
when choosing and ruling o'er old Second Street

'Till in come the house fleas with itchy sharp bites
and distract the mad cats on Holloween nights
    and send them in circles
        around and around
'till all of the creatures go back underground
to escape the loud ruckus and make it all cease
and regain some semblance of Second Street peace.

So lock up your grannies and toss out the key,
count all of the wee ones wherever they be
    and stuff them with cake
        'till they stagger to bed
then board up the windows aft' all prayers are said,
hold tight to your sweetie and make not a sound,
and neverly, *everly* go to downtown.

PART TWO

DOWN THE DAYS

IN A MOMENT OF PRAYER

Seven geese rise over a factory
near where I drive
in a state of limbo.
A restless night led to a peaceful morning
when I contemplated the loss of a friend
and my struggles to survive.
Like geese I want to live and fly
away from troubles on warm currents of air,
and I pray for resolution
to see the geese shift positions,
trying to define their formation,
giving to the moment
when they form their migration V
and all is perfect by design.

FRIENDLY DANCER

As I cover myself with moonlight
she dances
siren of my dreams
she floats
on delicate glass sneakers
gliding ever closer
to my soul as
she calls
every moment growing
ever closer until
she slips away
in daylight,
still always my friend,
still always a mystery to me.

PED MALL POET

stillness of late afternoon
skies colored gold
islands of flowers
and greenery
just past the gallery
a fountain and reflections
bubbling conversations
people sit on a painted bench
a sandwich shared
just outside a bar
a crumpled scrap of paper
in my back pocket
verses gather in my head
seagulls circling overhead
draw inspirations higher
a mural of blues and yellows
images added by passengers
life in the city captured
and hung on the wall
of a transit station
evening departures flashed on-screen
strangers say hello to nightfall
the ped mall waits for neon lights
when a princess dances in shadows
in the arms of her muse
I call it love

FROM A RIVER EXCURSION
TO A WINTER BEACH

My long-time association with Writers on the Avenue has given me many memories, from meeting others at an office for Artists in Action to Duffy De France giving me a tour of the Muscatine riverfront to many other activities in this group. Two events stand out where members shared good writing and fun.

The Riverboat Cruise

Once I took a summer night excursion on the Kent Feeds River Boat with Writers on the Avenue. Dick Stahl was there, and the highlight of the cruise was Duffy De France playing her banjo. As the boat went down the river we sang old songs and read our poems, the Iowa shoreline of the Mississippi at our side. That night the river cast a spell on me, and onboard I felt great creative energy as we shared our works.

In the dark, I was enthralled with the Mississippi, a mysterious presence, moving ever onward. The trees on the shoreline were silhouettes. My thoughts were filled with thoughts of Mark Twain and other great explorers. I was filled with a sense of awe, thinking that we were taking our own journeys of discovery in those few hours, connecting with a river many of us see each day.

I don't remember what poems Dick Stahl read that night, but I must note that he has written many great poems about the river, and poems about its bluffs. Fellow poets and I have told each other, that surely most local poets have written about the river. It's a great presence in our lives.

A Winter Beach Party

I remember one cold afternoon in February a beach party held inside the Muscatine Art Center. Some of us sat on blankets and talked. We took our turns and stood at a podium and read our poems. Friends Duffy DeFrance, Mary Kay Lane, and Tony Ledjte were there, and I've always enjoyed their works. A few hours, well spent, took me to a warmer place.

Writers on the Avenue has hosted many other activities for fellow writers and the community. Although we sit alone to write, there are many opportunities for writers to come together.

Iowa River
Photograph by Pat Bieber

THE SOUND OF RAIN

In summer
it silences
the roar of
lawn mowers
the buzz of
chain saws
the rat-a-tat-tat of
jack hammers
and
the breeze
strokes song
out of
chimes.

LOST

Dirty dishes in the sink,
Beds unmade, clothes unwashed;
Smell of fish lingering long,
Bits of fluff in carpet pile,
Children whining underfoot;
Erotica, where have you gone?

THE CEMETERY

is a lively
place today
chain saws
rip through
the remains of
hundred year old trees
backhoes grab
handfuls of history
to drop into the
waiting maws of
giant dump trucks
scents of sawdust and
sap mingle with
the sour tang of
diesel exhaust on the palate
in little bubbles of
silence families survey
the carnage of tumbled
tombstones the tornado
left behind as it
savaged the town
consuming homes
shops garages cars but
failing to claim
a single new resident for
this place

Winner, first place, Writers on the Avenue poetry contest 2008

FOR BOBBY

Remember me when I have forgotten you.

When I misplace my keys,
   tell me where they are.

When I lose my way home
   find me and take me there.

When I no longer know your name,
   speak to me of mine.

When I forget to care for myself,
   see to my needs tenderly.

And when I have lost all that I am,
   all that I was,
      all that I would have been,

Then please,
   please,
   please,
   in the name of God and all that you hold holy,
Remember me when I have forgotten you.

Author's note: This is the poem I read at my very first Writers on the
Avenue meeting. I don't know if the other members were aware of my
shaky voice and hands, but I certainly was! The welcoming reception and
helpful comments on this and all my other writing and writing projects have
kept me coming back for over twenty years. -G.O.

Jeff Boldt

LIFE FROM MY BACK PORCH

From my rocker on my back porch I watch the community of birds that call my backyard home. A few years ago we put some wooden birdhouses up on an old clothesline pole and the birds have in fact made them home. Over the years the birdhouses have become weathered and run down, which I guess makes me a birdhouse slumlord. But the birds use them despite their disrepair, and I have had hours of delight watching them go about their day.

The occupants of our little wooden shacks are wrens. They fly in and out, always improving the place with fresh straw or twigs that they like. They are very busy creatures and I have watched little chicks grow and eventually leave the nest. I have "aww"ed as a mother brought back worms and other food to feed to her children (or childwren).

There are other birds that frequent our backyard. Robins with their beautiful colored breasts wander around saying, "Look at me and my beauty. I am a pretty bird." That is until a cardinal rests on the fence and says, "Oh, yeah? Look how colorful I am." Blackbirds come around and cause mischief. They light on the birdhouses only to be forced away by the wrens. Those wrens are very territorial. I have seen a squirrel wander up the pole only to have his curiosity dive-bombed by the protective wrens. He meandered up the pole but scurried back down it.

Nature seems to have provided well for all the creatures she encompasses. Even the birds manage to exist through wind and weather, heat and storm, and continue to care for their young and avoid danger. As I have sat through the years and watched my feathered friends, I see their intelligence, a sense of purpose, a communal spirit. I have concluded that birds are actually smart, leading me to wonder why we call the less adept among us "birdbrains." Knowing some of these people, I find that an insult to the birds.

Why is it humans were allowed to evolve to the top of the food chain? Humans are the only species on earth that is so destructive. No other species kills thousands of its own kind in wars. No other species is destroying the environment in which we live. No other species pollutes our waterways and adversely affects so many other species as man. Perhaps we are the species of "birdbrains." When a bird does something stupid, do the other birds call him a "manbrain?"

These are the things I think about while rocking my way to ornithological enlightenment.

Judy Chapman

I HAD TO SAY GOODBYE TODAY

Some of us are lucky enough to have the honor of having close relationships with animals throughout our lifetimes. I truly believe that dogs and cats are our Heavenly Father's special gift to us; they give us unconditional love, asking nothing in return.

Three weeks ago I had to have my very special cat, Prince Charming, put down. Don't laugh, he was a very charming and gentle pet. My daughter and granddaughter gave him to me. We went to the Humane Society where they put you in a room with a lot of cats and you pick out the one you want. Well, it wasn't me who did the picking, it was Prince. He proceeded to jump on my lap and take possession. He purred and rubbed and didn't let any other cats near. Not in a bullying way, but in an "I love you, please take me home" way. Needless to say, he was the one I walked out the door with.

We bonded immediately. His gentleness and loving ways were extraordinary. One of my favorite things was when he would nose my blankets and I would lift them; then he would go under and we would cuddle the rest of the night. He was generous with gifts. He was an indoor-outdoor cat, so quite often I would find gifts of mice or small birds distributed in hallways or corners. He really was generous.

We had eight wonderful years together. Then all of a sudden Prince started acting sick, and he had never done that. He lay around not moving. We were going to take him to the vet the next morning when he disappeared.

I did not see him for two days. We searched all over. I was sure he had gone off to die, and I felt traumatized. Then, the next morning, I looked on the patio and there he was! He wasn't moving, and I called the vet immediately. My grandson and I got him in the cat carrier and took him to the vet.

47

The vet examined Prince and I was given the devastating news that he had liver disease. She told me that if she were me, she would put him down so he didn't suffer anymore. Up until that moment I had been fooling myself with thoughts of *the doctor will help him* and *he'll be okay*. Then reality hit me.

Moments like these are indelibly etched in my heart: the remaining minutes that I got to spend with him. I will remember every nuance, every moment after the injection was given until the last breath. Time flew by while they gave him the injection and my heart was breaking. I was cuddling him, and within seconds they said, "He's gone."

They left me alone for a few minutes and I could still feel him. I could still feel his warmth and love, and my heart did break. I hugged and cried and felt the closeness of a wonderful essence that had shared my life and would never be forgotten.

When I got home I immediately removed his perch from the window so it was not there to remind me every second of every day. That would help some, but many times a day I am reminded of my friend. *Oh, I have to feed him*, I think. *There he is lying on the couch. Oh, he's jumping up on my lap. There he is, lying close to my feet. Oh, Prince, not another mouse!*

I believe that we will be reunited with our special pets in heaven. There must be a better name than *pet*. That word just doesn't resonate.

Editor's note: This piece was written in January 2018 in response to that month's word challenge. The words given were bouquet, joy, happiness, nightmare, resolution, begin, handy, and splendiferous. –M.U.

OUR JOURNEY

On the wall in my bedroom is a sampler that I made several years ago. I heard these words and they kept running through my mind. The words struck me as so important that I wanted something close that would keep reminding me of them. My brain usually seems to live by the old adage, "Out of sight, out of mind," and this was too important to forget.

The sampler reads, "Relish life as you live it. Find joy in the journey." I'm going to write that again and you think about each word. "Relish life as you live it. Find joy in the journey."

There are two words that stand out: *relish* and *joy*. The dictionary states that relish is "pleasurable appreciation of anything; to take pleasure in; like, enjoy." I think that you should go further. It's like the best bouquet of roses that you've ever smelled, or the best chocolates that you've ever had in your life and you can't stop eating them. Remember the most wonderful moment in your life; maybe it was holding your first child, and you don't want to forget one second of those moments. That is how you should relish your life. Get every nuance, every good thing out of each moment of your life that you can.

The next word is joy and everyone thinks, "I know what that means," but do they? The dictionary states, "The emotion of great delight or happiness caused by something exceptionally good or satisfying; keen pleasure; elation." You'll notice that joy is caused by something exceptionally good. Is there a lot of that today or are there bad things waiting to happen? Watching the news before going to bed could cause nightmares. Nowadays it is like evil is waiting around every dark corner ready to leap out and kill somebody. We are hearing more and more about raids and murders by terrorists. But guess what? There are more who would like to find happiness, peace, and joy and relish life as they live it if they know how.

Make a resolution that you will begin to relish life. Start now and you will discover that you are living a positive life. It will feel really good, maybe even joyful. Remember, get every nuance of every precious moment that is special to you. Soon you will find that you automatically turn towards the good and joyful.

Sounds easy, doesn't it? You just have to be careful and think positive; look for the good. Oh, if it were only that easy. On my sampler are some of the good things in life: butterflies, birds, flowers, and hearts. I didn't put anything negative on it because that would have ruined the message it was giving.

But our lives have a way of taking some unexpected turns and spills. Oops, that wasn't supposed to happen. All of a sudden life isn't so handy or attainable anymore. Things have changed towards the negative. Now I have to go job hunting all the time. All I get done is look for job openings or try to get an interview. Or I'm always sitting waiting in the doctor's office, Dr. So & So for this illness and Dr. So & So for that illness. Will this never end? Or how do you find joy when your world is filled with pain? Pain literally takes over your world, day and night. Every time you want to do something you have to think, "Am I going to be able to do this? Will it hurt too much?" It becomes very hard to relish life and find joy under countless situations that take all of your time.

One of the ways that I have seen people conquer their problems is those who have found the answer for themselves. Instead of giving in to their ailments, they have reached out to help others. These people have found the secret. Forget about yourselves and remember the ones who need your help. The people I know who live by this creed are some of the happiest people I have ever seen. I don't know if they have forgotten their problems or not, but they are ready to set them aside and help their fellow man.

Each of us has to find his answer to this problem and get on the path to being able to relish life and find joy.

There are many things in our lives that we can't control, but how we react to our journey through life is under our control. We are going to have a splendiferous journey.

THE SMELL OF ART

I open my Dick Blick catalog

suddenly

the smell of art bursts

into a brilliant shiny plume

where my aria resonates.

I must knead the clay to a musty crust

beneath my fingernails,

feed diluent vapor trails beyond

the scratch of a brush stroke,

grind the cedar shavings from my drawing pencil

until exhilaration meets exhaustion.

WILD BLUE

Moist surface cracks breath —

Deep rooted talons descend

Of wild blue asters

Anna Counter

LETTING GO

How do you let go? Is there a special way to let go of different areas of your life when you begin to feel that you have assimilated all the knowledge a situation has to offer, learned all that you can, and feel the need to move on?

Letting go of a way of life, a way of thinking, a relationship is never the easiest thing you will ever do, and yet many times you become aware, consciously, that in order to continue growing to your fullest potential you need to move on.

Sometimes this need forces you to trust in yourself to the point of kicking the props out from under the secure life that you have formed, and holding your nose as you jump, trusting that a safety net will be there.

If the change involves a relationship, you learn that the only person that you can ever change is yourself, and sometimes that change involves going on alone.

To continue learning, sometimes you must change your classroom. But this is always a choice, and you may elect to jump back into a comfortable situation after testing the new waters and finding the unfamiliar not to your liking.

Above all, you cannot blame others for intolerable situations that you have had a part in creating.

You cannot answer for others, but only for your own need to grow and learn, for that is a major part of life: growing and learning. The world becomes new and exciting, if just a little frightening as you face new challenges that stretch your mind and heart to as-yet-unexplored levels of understanding.

Can you allow your spirit to cherish each new day, each new situation, each new relationship for the ultimate growth it offers?

Can you allow your dreams and your beliefs to become your guides and mentors, and follow them to the limits of your capabilities?

Never regret the happenings of the past. The events, the relationships that occurred were what made you the person you are today.

Letting go is essentially the same for any situation or relationship that you have grown beyond.

Even if you are ready for change, it is seldom an easy task. But in letting go you are doing a service not only to yourself, but also to the other parties by allowing them to move on as well.

SLEEPLESS AT MIDNIGHT

It's not located on any map. It has no name.
You cannot simply go there at will.
But on a moonless November night,
when it's not quite fall and not quite winter,
and the wind moans through dark pines outside your window,
and if you're still awake and restless at midnight,
you may find your way to the lonely place.

On a night such as this you will not find
the peaceful rest you crave, but only a dark journey
into used-to-be's and never-were's, into unfulfilled wishes
and prayers never answered, or sometimes, worse, answered.
Into dreams that were trampled, places never visited,
things never tried, and the bleakness of failures.
Of loves never consummated,
friendships that died of neglect.

Disturbing thoughts pour from your mind like ants
from an anthill, each bearing its dark gift.
As you encounter them, one by one,
scabs are torn off old wounds, unresolved
and still festering, and haunting fears, again,
cower you into submission.
Old hates flame up like revived embers.
Old loves taunt with what might have been —
promises never kept and loving things left unsaid,
and too much said that caused pain.
Your breath quickens and a sweaty coldness
sets you tossing until you leave your bed
in whipped surrender
to find remedy to plug your ungoverned mind.

It's not located on any map. It has no name.
You cannot simply go there at will.
But on a moonless November night,
when it's not quite fall and not quite winter,
and the wind moans through dark pines outside your window,
and if you're still awake and restless at midnight,
you may find your way to the lonely place.

Editor's note: This was another response to a WOTA word challenge. The given words were possibility, surprising, stocking, marginal, insidious, and supporter. Anna packed them all into a small but pithy piece. –M.U.

DISTINCT POSSIBILITY

It is surprising what the human race is capable of. I never cease to be amazed and proud when I watch my fellow humans in their ongoing attempt to grow beyond themselves.

I, too, am engaged in the day-to-day struggle to rise above my baser nature. Speaking only for myself, my success is many times marginal to say the least. Fitting my baser nature into the accepted mold of real humanity is much like pulling on an orthopedic stocking over a wet noodle. I pull and push and try to fit it on right, and yet in many instances, I bend here and lop over there. For every silly millimeter I gain I must fight, at times nearly to the death, to force myself to accept the growth that I feel is so essential to the human I wish to become.

I periodically shore up my progress with a supporter. I like to think of it as faith: faith in a Creator, faith in my fellow man, and lastly faith in myself.

This faith has carried me through many adversities, most of which were definite learning experiences. Many times personal gain, monetary rewards, or personal dislikes make themselves known loud and clear, attempting in their insidious ways to sneak around and force me back into a mold — the mold that I have many times clawed my way out of with torn and bleeding fingernails.

If I have learned one thing in my life, it is that life is neither good nor bad; life is life, a state of being to be lived to the best of my ability. I have kicked my own butt so many times that I sport a permanent callus, and I'm quite familiar with the feel of one or both feet in my mouth, but this is learning and after all, we are essentially here to learn through experience. So learn to love and enjoy life no matter what it brings. Just remember that there is so much more to the real you than what you are dealing with right now.

"I didn't write the Great American Novel...
I wrote the GREATEST American novel."

Daniel Roberts

Kimberly Dickens

LOST POWER

My son pretends to plant a garden.
He can imagine the dirt,
the sun, the water,
the passing from today into tomorrow.
When all his pebbles are suddenly fruit,
he sees fairies in the clover
and the King of Ants on toadstool,
ready to invade.
His little hands bring a water can
just in time,
so the whole world parades.
He catches lightning bugs, dancing,
knowing they will obey
and light the corner of his room
where angled shadows tend to stray.

MODERN ALCHEMY

There was something in the water today.
Maybe just plastic residue, dust or decay.
Cried a lot, then
ran and made it on time. I had
found inspiration and wanted to bow to it.
Started to confess
everything I have done, and all the times
I did nothing.
Read Marlowe and thought I
understood myself,
deaf to angels and tired of waiting.

I am a Gen-X missionary
We knew
Sci-fi had it right, that the world should
be solid, one voice,
nothing Earth is alien and
I am not alone.

One cup International
decaf, vanilla bean latte and
I accept foreclosure for now.
There is truth and comedy
as you pull yourself
from a hole.
Everything is less impossible.
Found a kind of spirituality
in being a Transformer,
like coughing up hope or
a lead heart bending —
like coffee with
George Carlin and Douglas Copeland.

Judy Haskins

SEASONS ON THE FARM

I grew up in the township of Wilton Junction, Iowa, in the 1960s. Even though it was a small town, I was not allowed to go far from home; across the street to the neighbor's to play, to school, and occasionally downtown was about the extent of it. Yet, when we visited Grandma, my parents set me free for hours. The farm was the place of freedom and experiencing life.

Grandma, Grandpa, and two cousins lived on a farm west of Birmingham, Iowa. They had a little old two-story farmhouse with weathered siding, plastic on some of the windows, and bales of straw around the foundation to keep the wind from whistling through in the winter. It had one room upstairs and three down. With no running water, it was like the old days. The privy was about thirty feet away, and the milk can in the corner of the kitchen held the drinking water. We all drank from the same ladle and raced to get the first drink of the fresh, ice-cold well water. We were pretty healthy, amazingly enough. Two wood stoves heated the little house, but the cook stove was gas, one modern convenience. They had hogs, chickens, a mean rooster that would fly at anyone passing by, the cow named Knothead, and Bob Dog.

My favorite place on the farm was the timber. No matter what the time of year, there were always things to do and learn. Early fall was the most beautiful time with splashes of color like a painter's palette. There were walnuts and hickory nuts to retrieve. We were like monkeys squatting around the treasure, sharing Grandpa's hammer or impatiently using a rock to break the hard shells and eat the treats inside. Later in the fall, the crisp dried leaves and twigs crackled underfoot.

Grandma had the absolute best hill for sledding. We shared one runner sled and a couple scoop shovels. I remember sitting Indian-style in the scoop, holding on to the handle for dear life, and being pushed down the hill. Having no steering ability, inevitably I would hit a bump, the handle bopped me in the head, and I went tumbling. I laughed so hard my cheeks hurt. The smoke from the wood burners called me to get warm. Even today, that smell takes me back to Grandma's.

Eventually, everything came to life. In the spring we hunted for the biggest and most sponge-like morel mushrooms. I didn't want to eat them after seeing the bugs inside as Grandma cleaned them. Little did I know I would grow up to love God's little gift and cook them exactly the way she did. The dogwood and redbud trees were in bloom, and so was Grandma's lilac bush by the driveway. The creek was flowing once again after the frigid winter months.

Summer was my favorite time. We stayed two weeks, and most of the days were spent in Grandma's wonderland. The sledding hill was also the ideal place to lie in the grass and shout out the countless shapes seen in the clouds. We could see the creek from the top of the hill. It was amazing to me that the flow of this humble stream could have etched such a curious path. A ten-foot wall of shale cut by the power struggle of land versus water was awesome and demonstrated the patience of nature. It seemed to be rushing from the shallow areas to the deeper, tranquil pools. The large stones aided our crossing as we tried not to get too muddy. I was tempted by the life in the pools, and my cousins challenged me to get out of my comfort zone. I caught the speedy minnows in a soup can, picked up a lobster-looking crawfish, and attempted to scale down a cliff. I felt strong and confident.

Eventually, we would journey back to the house for a sponge bath and a relaxing evening. At the end of the day, Mother Nature's choir would begin: the locusts would start, next the high pitched crickets. Then, as it grew dark, the tree frogs and pond frogs would chime in, and soon the bull frogs would sound off like baritones. Finally the hoot owls would call good night. The night sky filled with a myriad of twinkling jewels. Now that is true beauty.

Ron Lackey

THE FLUFFY EXPERIENCE

Times were tough and there wasn't a lot of money to go around, but I always tried to save up and do a little something special for the kids on Christmas. Christmas is a great time of year to share caring and love with family and friends, but it's a little different for a child. It's different when you're a parent, but sometimes the gift gives back and makes it all worth it.

My son, Lakota, has always loved comedy, a good joke, or a prank that he can pull off, so I thought it would be great to take him to a comedy concert. He's a big fan of Gabriel Iglesias, so, why not? Gabriel is a clean comic, and Lakota was still in high school at the time. For Christmas, I gifted him a pair of tickets for a show the following March at the Adler Theater in Davenport, Iowa. It was a few months away, but he was thrilled, and so was I since he asked me to go with him. I ain't gonna lie. I wanted to go too, but I told him that he could take anybody.

So, March rolls around and off to the event Lakota and I go. Anybody who knows me understands that no matter where I go, I always get there ridiculously early. No joke. I wanted to make sure we could get good parking, get to our seats, blah, blah, blah, just excuses to justify my anxiety-riddled fear of being late. I think we were two hours early. We walked around the lobby and looked at the art, made sure we knew where the bathrooms were and where the box office was so I could show my internet passes, and sat in just about every seat in the pavilion while we waited. I suppose we could have left and gotten something to eat, but we didn't want to leave our comfy seats and pole position getting into the venue. So we waited and exchanged chit chat about home life, teen driving, his sister, Chloee, and other general father-son bonding subjects. Oh, and the fact that we were two hours early. That came up as well. I'm working on that. I really am.

Sooner or later people started coming into the venue and the line behind us became longer, the box office opened, I showed our internet tickets, and we stood in another line in front of red velvet ropes. On the other side was the main lobby of the theater. It was very similar to the lobby of a movie theater. After the ropes were lowered, we were able to proceed to what I found out was a bar. Lakota and I passed on getting a beverage and decided to find our seats. We broke away from the herd that was heading towards the watering hole.

There were ushers, but their services needed not to be rendered. I booked the tickets late and our seats were easy to find as they were three rows from the back wall. The Adler occupancy is 2400 with a balcony so there isn't a bad seat in the joint, but the seats themselves are terrible. The place must have been built around 1900 when the average person was five foot five and weighed a buck fifty. Lakota and I are both big boys, so I let him have the aisle seat and whoever was on my left side could deal with my overflow.

Lakota and I kept waiting and the seats started to fill. We let people by who were looking for their seats. Everyone around us was drinking, loud, and having a good time, and this was before the curtain went up. I could smell the beer, and there was a gang of good ole boys and their girlfriends behind us. The couple next to me was talking about their favorite drinks and the fellow half of the two sat next to me, double-fisting a set of Solo cups.

In a poor effort to apologize for my overflow I told the young fellow, "These seats aren't very fluffy friendly, are they?" Gabriel Iglesias' nickname is "Fluffy" because of his size, and I thought it would be a great ice breaker. Mocking chuckles came from the good ole boys behind us. I'm sure their girlfriends were impressed.

"I'm aware of the seating" was what I got back. Enough said.

The lights went down and the show started. The opening act was Gabriel's best friend, Martin Moreno. Out the door went the clean show.

"If you brought your kids you might want to get them the [bleep] out of here. Gabriel's show is clean, but mine's not." I'm paraphrasing, but that was Martin's opening line. I didn't get my kid out of there and Martin's set was funny as hell. It was a good time, and I'm sure that Lakota was no stranger to the vulgar verbiage from the stage. Poor parenting, but I was a cool dad for a bit, and then Gabriel performed.

I can't remember exactly when the intermission came. I think it was halfway through Gabriel's set, but I'm not sure. During intermission, the herd went to the watering hole again and the entire auditorium population packed itself in front of the bar. I was going to get water for Lakota and myself, but the sea of drunks kept undertowing me out to sea, so I gave up and we took our seats and waited. Deja vu, we let people pass as they went to their seats. Again, the dude to my left was double-fisting his favorite beverage and the show continued.

Continue the show did, for almost an extra hour. Gabriel announced that he was going to present new material as well as the old. He asked the crowd if we would mind spending extra time to hear the new material and of course there was clamorous affirmation. The show went on, and on.

Normally an elongated performance from a comedian is a great thing. However, there was alcohol involved, which meant an extra hour of drinking for my friend to the left and my new buddies behind us. Ladies and gentlemen, there was trouble brewing in River City.

The guy next to me started hiccuping. "Are you alright?" his female companion asked him. I should have known this guy was gonna be trouble. He was one of these turn-of-the-last-century wraiths, a twenty-something hipster in tight jeans weighing the buck fifty I wrote about earlier. Not skinny enough to keep my overflow off of his leg, though. He started hiccuping harder, placing his hand in front of his mouth.

Yeah, he wasn't hiccuping, he was throwing up beer foam. Essentially, he was puking, blocking it with his hand, and swallowing it back down. After each catch and stifle, he wiped his hand on his right thigh where my overflow was, so he was not only wiping his beer puke on his pants, but my pants too. What was I gonna do, cause a scene in front of my kid? Should I have blasted the fool in the mouth? What is the appropriate move when someone is wiping their beer puke on you? Looking back, I should have thrown an elbow.

The fun didn't end. Amid the guffaws and yuck yucks, one of the girl pals of the good ole boys behind Lakota and me decided to puke. There were a couple of early warning heaves and then splash on the carpet floor, followed by a chorus of "oh nos" and "awe, mans." Call it Karma or Divine Intervention, either way, I became a believer.

The show went on despite the tribulations of the last three rows. It was a good show. I was glad I went with my son. I was glad that we were close to the exit. I was glad that we were first to our car. I was glad that we were among the first out of the parking lot. I was glad we went. I was glad to have had the Fluffy experience.

Jason Liegois

REST HOLDS
(A Kayfabe Tale)

I was just a kid
looking for action
on The Tube
that dominated my attention
when pro wrestling hooked me
like Lou Thesz used to hook.
I loved the big bumps
the spots from Up High
and the soap opera drama aimed at men
and those who would be men.
Some of the wrestlers were
60-minute men,
the ones who could wrestle
All Night Long.
Those matches were packed
with bumps and high spots and
The Big Finish
at the end.
It was an inevitability, especially in
those 60-minute Broadway matches,
that at some point,
one wrestler would get the other wrestler
in a
head lock

arm lock
leg lock
and the other guy or gal
would lay there on the floor,
occasionally trying to
writhe out of their
Iron Grasp.
And they'd always shriek and yell
in agony.
I always wondered as a kid
how they could take that
level of punishment.
Later, however, as the veil of
Kayfabe
was lifted before Y2J was a thing,
I found out those were the times in a match
when they were catching their breath.
They even called them "rest holds."
I never held it against them, though.
There's plenty of times in my own life
where I need some rest holds to get by.

CLOSING DOORS

Down the grey hall, fluorescents
flickering more and more as the clock hands
drag
I walk past the doors.
Some are French, others
industrial with piston handles,
others are American Revival
(when is that coming?)
Years back, I remember
that all the doors were open,
and you were able to walk in.

There were doors that led to long
flights of staircases, or
balance-beam narrow bridges.
Some of the doors had come from bank vaults,
so it took my shoulder and my bulk
to get it open.
Sometimes I ducked my head behind the door
and found empty desks or rows of kids playing all board games
I'd gotten tired of when
I was 5.
I walked into the occasional vault door
or the one where I had
to wrestle it open or climb a hyperangle hill.

As I look around now,
something has slowly changed.
Every year, I try the handle of a door and find it locked.
Every year, I discover a couple more doors locked, or chained
shut.

There are a few metal doors that
have been freshly welded shut,
the gun-grey solder ice-hot to the touch,
the door handles smashed.
Nowadays, I'd say whenever I stalk the hall,
half of the doors can't be opened
for one reason or the other.

I've realized those closings can't be helped.
You can only leave the doors open for so long
before closing up shop.
The only door that doesn't seem ready for the lock
is the one at the end of the hall.
It doesn't appear to have an actual door, just an ornately carved
oak doorjamb and
ink darkness bleeding out from it.
I always walk down there to the end, but I've never looked in and
never walked in.

Maybe later.

Maybe I'll have to, when all of the doors
are locked and I'm not able to open
anything else.
Every time I have fewer doors.
Usually that makes me sad to tears, makes my nerves raw.
Recently, I've begun
wondering if what I will feel when the time comes
will be simply relief.
Or maybe I'll be able to pick a few locks
by then.

WHAT MADE ME START WRITING AGAIN

In the movies—and in plenty of novels—there usually is some sort of turning point scene, one moment when the protagonist's life pivots and moves in a new direction. It is one moment of clarity after which that person's life has forever and irrevocably changed.

It wasn't like that for me. In looking through old word document files in my "fiction" folder, I see several starts and stops among the last decade. Some of them I talked about before; others fell stillborn after a few months of typing and procrastination. Then there was the anonymous blog I ran for a few months somewhere in the past decade. It really didn't have any focus except as an emotional purge, and I eventually decided that I needed to shut it down to avoid any static in my real life.

But like St. Augustine once prayed during his youth, "Oh, Lord, make me chaste . . . but not yet."

I think things started to coalesce in my head right around 2010. That was an interesting year, to be frank. I'm not planning to get into it here, but there was a bit of turmoil and uncertainty in my professional life. For a brief moment, I had a dream of becoming a college writing instructor full-time rather than teaching for a couple thousand per class. I say a dream rather than a goal because I only had a vague idea of what the job involved and how I would achieve it. After a few years and different circumstances, I set that idea aside.

Recently, I had a chance to read through a notebook I was writing in for about three months or so back in 2010. I tried to read all of it, but it was a cursive scribble stream of consciousness. It was lists and lists of various things I was both positively and negatively obsessed with, among other things.

In reading through that notebook, I think I did what we used to call in journalism "burying the lede." Others, like writing teachers, might call it an implied main idea. What I think I was describing in those entries was being addicted to distraction.

Anything I could use to procrastinate from doing anything, thinking about anything, I'd be into.

There was a time in my life that the distractions would dominate me. For several years of my life, it seemed being entertained, being satisfied in whatever way, was more important than anything else that wasn't my family.

Around 2007-2010, right after I moved back to Muscatine, I really started heavily surfing some backwaters and little-known areas on the Internet. It may have given me a couple of writing ideas, but mostly I was looking, as I normally did, for a distraction.

Back in those days, I often read the website Postsecret. It allows people to anonymously send postcards on which they write their deepest and darkest secrets that they would not tell anyone. Around 2010, I read a postcard on the site that said "I lived at home until I was 37. Then I changed everything. It's not too late."

For me, that had two effects. First, it gave me hope that it really wasn't too late to get started (or restarted, whatever you want to classify it as) on my dreams of becoming a writer of novels. I always heard about people like Frank McCourt writing their debut books when they were in their 50s, 60s, or beyond.

Secondly, it was a prod in the butt, something that said yeah, if you're about as old as this guy, why not get started now?

So, did Liegois actually take the postcard's advice and move forward?

As I said, nothing that dramatic happened. Someone's personality and habits—at least, not my own—are not things that can change direction like a fighter aircraft or speedboat. The process more resembles having to maneuver a jumbo jet or mega-tanker a few degrees off course.

Did my life actually change?

Over time, yes.

Soon after, I began to reminisce about some of my days in journalism, what was happening to newspapers in this country, and the weirdness of the time specifically around 2008. Going by my computer file history, I'd have to say that I started to play around with the idea of doing a journalism/political thriller around 2011. By 2013-14, ironically when I was taking one last adventure into journalism, I finalized a rough draft.

It was somewhere around 2013 that I began keeping track of the word count that I was getting done on a daily and weekly basis. Although not effective at first, I think that having to keep track of what I am actually writing or revising has helped me be accountable to myself and have goals to work for, even though I rarely have weeks where I meet my daily goals throughout the entire week.

It took me until 2016 to get another draft of the piece I was now calling *The Holy Fool* done; I had to do a little bit of cutting to trim it to under 100,000 words. By 2017 I had revised it into its current form and had begun shopping it around to agents and publishers. I'm now awaiting the publishing process.

Also by 2016, I had worked up the courage/willingness/ audacity to write a novel about someone who played a sport I hadn't played myself since elementary school and located in both a state I hadn't lived in since I was five and another country I had never visited, much less lived in. However, I was ready for the challenge, and by the next year, I already had a rough draft in the bag for my next project. I've gotten deep into the revising process with it, and I'm liking how my refined techniques have sped the writing process along.

Would I say that I have fully defeated my addiction to distraction and procrastination? Not by any means. I still exhibit those behaviors today, in doses both big and small. However, I've started to be able to manage this addiction to the point where I've become a productive writer. And I want to stay that way. I'm not exactly sure how long I have or how many books I have in me, but I want to make that time count.

Editor's note: *The Holy Fool: A Journalist's Revolt* by Jason Liegois was published by Biblio Publishing in January 2019. —M.U.

"It's the perfect first anniversary for my
first book: paper for my second one!"

Daniel Roberts

Denise Smith

EBONY CROSSES

Telephone poles like totems,
    standing tall and proud.
Diminishing with distance
    then fade into the clouds.

They look like ebony crosses
    extending to infinite days,
The sun sets far beyond them
    in shadows of purple haze.

As the gentle breeze whispered
    I looked upon this art.
The row of ebony crosses
    strummed upon my heart.

THE SWEETHEART ROSE

I looked upon
　　the tiny sweetheart rose
　　　　and saw its possibilities.

It began to open
　　revealing hidden layers
　　　　that coiled continually.

As time went on,
　　more petals opened,
　　　　revealing more layers.

It bloomed where it was planted
　　inside the vase, though
　　　　I knew that it would die.

Still its sweet scent
　　and endless layers
　　　　gave me pleasure for days.

PART THREE

NEW VOICES

Robin Abbott

WHEN ART MEETS SCIENCE
IN A FIFTH GRADER

Even her name was something I'd never heard before: Taft Utermohle. Almost as if she made it up. A little precursor of the creativity that was her business. No other art teachers before or after are at all memorable for me. Art in particular is not memorable for me. But she approached art as a science, which flipped a switch in my psyche.

She was stylish, unafraid. She owned it. She had wild hair and wore long flowy skirts in earth-tones and big, chunky jewelry. Her style was sophisticated bohemian. At eleven years old, I had no idea what "sophistication" was, nor "bohemian." But, in sleepy suburban Timonium, Maryland, it was noticeable. One noticed.

"See the negative space," she proselytized. "Look at the area that *isn't* the object you are drawing. Draw that." She had all sorts of tricks to short-circuit my brain. "Draw it upside-down. Draw the white areas of light. Everything around them is a variation on the light."

Most importantly, best of all, she introduced me to the idea that there were two halves of the brain. The mind wasn't just this churning glob of input and output. The left side of the brain names and judges and categorizes things. The right side sees things without labeling them; it makes connections between seemingly unrelated things. As an adult, I know that this is an over-simplification. Taft made concrete the abstract idea that you could see the same thing a hundred different ways, depending on what part of your brain was doing the observing. I was a logical, left-brain-living fifth-grader and she showed me the steps to access the right side of my brain.

I was new to school that year, having moved to town in November. The kids in the class had all known each other since kindergarten, and they had no need to befriend me. So I had a lot of free time on my hands to play with the assignments I learned in Taft's art class. I spent one Saturday drawing my favorite teddy bear upside down. When I was done, the likeness was impressive for an inexperienced eleven-year-old. I was impressed with myself, which was an unfamiliar feeling, given the kick to the ego that having no friends repeatedly produces. It was lovely to feel good about myself.

Taft introduced me to neurology, which is the direction my life continued in after fifth grade. I still function most comfortably in words — labeling things, naming and judging them. But Taft also taught me that art makes consciousness leap to the right side of the brain, so that the eyes can see things as they really are. The more often my brain can make that leap, the easier it becomes. I can observe the idea, the abstract, the emotion from a more passive perspective to see what is really there. The actual shapes, the spaces between, the connections and the essence of a thing. Of a person. Of an idea. When the brain slaps a label on a thing — "This is a house. That is a car" — it's hard to *imagine* the thing in actuality. The brain cannot conjure the very thing it sees, because it also sees all the other "cars" or "houses" of its past. It becomes impossible to transfer it to paper as it is. The intermediary left-brain overlays its label and shape of how a "house" or a "car" ought to be.

But to escape labels is to create art. An artist sees the qualities of what is there, the components that make it up. The artist's brain explodes it, deconstructs it, and reassembles it — on paper, in clay, in words, exactly as it is. Everything is new. Nothing has been seen before.

FIRST-BORN

I hold my first-born close to me
Sensing new responsibility.
How can I be equipped, I ask,
To carry out this fearsome task
Until he walks free.

I gave his life to him
Thinking not in lover's whim
I copied a life who I must lead.
Oh, give me strength enough, I plead.

I hear his crying in the night.
Seek him out in dimmed light.
Satisfy his raging thirst
Watching new sun rays burst
Upon my first-born son.

FOGGY BRAIN

I lie repressed by foggy brain
Trying to think of one refrain
That lies covered by this dust.
This cloudy cover so unjust
Its arid fields cry for rain.

Just ago I walked upright
Under sun's shining light
But now suppressed I lie
With foggy brain.

It is for you who sense my fog
To set me up on stool or log
And give me drink from cup or well
Until you sense the cloud dispel
From foggy brain.

Editor's note: This was Alan's response to the word list for March 2018. The given words were queen, power, sestina, gerbils, saber-tooth, lordosis, open, hilarious, fidelity, apricot, and 10%. You can see the group was feeling particularly feisty in February, with that selection, but Alan rose to the challenge magnificently. – M.U.

AN ORIGINAL TALE

Once upon a time in an ocean far away a small tribe of people lived on an island. Their king grew very old and died, leaving no heir to his throne. His wife died shortly after they were married. He mourned her the rest of his life. This tribe languished for years after the king's death. Their faces grew long. Their usual hilarity ceased to exist. Their fidelity to each other grew thin. In their anger neighbors often spat apricot pits at one another.

Though they longed for a ruler, no man or woman summoned the courage to sit on that empty throne. Then an old man who always wore a saber-tooth skin openly declared himself king. Afflicted with a severe case of lordosis, he lacked the power to sustain his claim. The people laughed him out of town back to his hut in the woods.

The children on the island made an eccentric man who lived on the far edge of their community, raised gerbils, wrote sestina poetry and brewed a strange beer, the object of their apricot pits. To their utter chagrin he never reacted angrily. He gathered all the pits, taking them behind his cottage. Some daring boys sneaked into the woods to watch what the man did with the pits. They saw him cracking and grinding, cracking and grinding. They more pits they spat the more he cracked and ground. The mystery deepened.

(Have I captured your attention, at least 10%?)

So, allow me to continue. One day a Dutch ship captain happened on the island. His crew was starving. They needed supplies. Someone told him to go to the eccentric man who welcomed him. On tasting the delicious paste the eccentric man made from the pits, the Dutch captain declared, "I must take this wonderful paste to my Queen." They quickly struck a bargain:

Dutch Delft and Dutch cigars for as much paste as the captain wanted.

He went to the coast and blew his horn. His emaciated crew aroused the pity of the islanders. Over the next weeks they nursed the crew back to health. In the meantime the islanders begged the eccentric man for permission to help him make more paste, which he gladly gave. He revealed his recipe of nuts and coconut plus the sweet syrup of some tree sap that formed his paste.

One day those boys I mentioned marched back and forth in front of the eccentric man's property shouting, "Here lives our new King. Here lives our new King."

Soon everyone joined the shout. On a bright sunny day they set a crown on his head and the eccentric man became an eccentric king who reigned many eccentric but happy years.

On leaving the captain vowed to return with ships of supplies and other goods for the islanders to express the crew's gratitude for the help they received. He proved the worth of his word.

The Queen hailed the captain and his treat. The captain's name was Klaas Van Kett. Somehow or other his treat became known as *banket*.

And now you know the origin of Dutch *banket* (marzipan, or almond paste) which you will find at many stores and Dutch bakeries in various Dutch communities such as Pella, Iowa.

Bob Bancks

WHAT'S IN A WORD?

It was past midnight in Farmer Bob's basement barn. Most of the animals were asleep or dozing. Cow 1 and Cow 2, the two milk cows, were relaxing in the loafing part of the barn, chewing a delicious wad of cud. Pig was snoring loudly in his sty. Cat was prowling, looking for Mouse. The bare bulb light hanging from the floor joist was dark. There was only a sliver of a moon outside which made the night almost whimsical. With high humidity and clear skies, it would be a dewy morning tomorrow.

The silence was broken when Dog jumped over the door with a ball of paper in his mouth.

"What's cha' got there, Dog?" asked Cat.

"I don't know. It's a ball of paper I found in the driveway. I think Farmer Bob threw it out of the pickup window on his way to the Country Jubilee Singers at the fair."

"The fair? What's that?"

"It's where humans go to show off their livestock and garden produce and flowers. They like to see how they compare with their friends and neighbors. Mrs. Bob competes in the needle work contest. She's into crewel and needle point. Whatever that is? "

Dog dropped the paper on the ground and flattened it out with his paw.

"Pull the string on the light. Maybe I can figure out what it says."

Cat reached with her claw and caught the long cord for the light, then jumped down from the top of the stanchion.

"How can you figure it out? You can't read. Let a cat do the reading."

Cat scanned the paper and said, "This is some kind of a word game. There are a bunch of words written on it. It says everyone should try and write a story using all the words. It's from a group called Writers on the Avenue. I think they are a group of wannabee writers who are good but don't want to quit their regular jobs and just write."

"I'll bet Farmer Bob tried and couldn't do it, so he just threw the paper away in disgust," said Dog.

"I can understand most of the words. There are just three I never heard of. They just mystify me," commented Cat. "Let's ask Cow 1 or Cow 2."

The pair traipsed over to the loafing shed which was attached to the side of the barn. Dog nudged Cow 1. She was silently chewing her cud and dozing at the same time. She woke up and let out a huge belch.

Dog held his paw over his nose and said, "My goodness, Cow 1, that smells awful. What did you have for dinner?"

"Oh some, corn, oats, soybean meal, and clover hay. I love clover hay. It tastes like caramel candy, but it gives me bad breath."

"You can say that again."

"It gives me bad breath."

"Gee, you really didn't have to say it again. It smells awful."

"Okay, let me swallow this cud and I'll be fine. What can I do for you and Cat?"

"I found this paper with these words on it. We don't know what three of them mean."

Cow 1 looked the paper and mooed, "Esoteric, cantankerous, anthology. Nope, can't help you on the first two. Anthology, isn't that something to do with growing corn?"

By this time Cow 2 had awakened and heard Cow 1. She scoffed and said, "No, you stupid cow, that's agronomy. I think it is the study of human history."

"Oh, that's not right. That's anthropology," replied Cow 1 as she turned to Dog and said, "Go ask Pig. He's smart. He'll know."

Dog and Cat went to the Pig's sty. He was dreaming of a big cool hog wallow and was all smiles.

Cat went right up to his ear and let out a "meow."

Pig woke up and snorted. "What do you two want?"

"We want to know what these three words mean," barked Dog.

Pig looked at the paper. He smiled again.

"Esoteric is a Canadian word meaning something that you fear because it's icky or gross. Here's how I break it down. Eh — so! Terribly icky. They just shortened it to esoteric. The next one is also Canadian. It's for a trucking company which hauls gasoline. You see, *can* stands for Canada, followed by *tanker*, which stands for a semi hauling gasoline. OUS means they haul gasoline to the US. Cantankerous. It is as simple as that. Now are there any more questions? Because I want to continue my beauty sleep."

"What about anthology?" cried Cat.

"Never heard of it. Let's try and figure it out. I'd say it has something to do with ants or maybe an Aunt Holly someone, but I'd stay with the ant theory. You know, ant hollow o gee! It must mean Gee! There's an ant mound in the hollow."

"Thank you, Pig, for explaining those words to us."

As Cat and Dog were returning to the center of the barn, Dog said to Cat, "I wish I could tell Farmer Bob what Pig said. I'll bet he'd really be happy and maybe give me a new bone."

Cat hissed back, "In your dreams, Dog. You better get some sleep before Rooster wakes up. I hate it when he crows. Sometimes I wish someone would have him for dinner."

Editor's note: Farmer Bob and his animal fables have become legendary in WOTA in recent years, but this entry demonstrates how inventive writers can be in including all the words from a challenge in their piece. –M.U.

"It's my novel's first birthday."

Daniel Roberts

Kathy Geren Christy

WENDING THROUGH THE MAZE

Stroking the silken sleepy Siamese kitten
as she curls up on my lap in her feline cocoon

Ideas remain phantoms in the attic of my mind

Similes, metaphors, swirling isms and ings
jumbled unformed meanings like Scrabble tiles
scattered on a formica kitchen table

Gazing out at the clouded autumnal scene
Stately silvery birches,
Brilliant cardinals on perches,
Raindrops clinging to branches, crystalline, pristine.

Visions emerge.
The birth of a poem.

Ralph Montrone

WHAT WEATHER

We have gone from a deep blue sky
    As the day passed by
To a warm humid hazy blue
    When night was due in late August.
It's time for the late summer cool wave.
    The dog days will still come
Like a predatory knave,
    As a late September or October bum.
We now have a hurricane
    Moving up the East Coast
Gaining strength as it does
    May it come and go quickly,
And not stall anymore.
    The weather can go from comfortable to prickly in a flash.
This is the new weather score, pitiless and brash.
    It will transform into something
    terrible and rash.
The cool spell in summer is welcome;
    The hurricane is not.
The question is not what hell have we caught,
    But what hell have we bought?

Monica Flink

GRETA GRAY

Greta Gray, a woman who refused to take her husband's last name because there was power in a double g-r name, was being haunted. Normally, this would be no problem for a witch like her. A few apple pips, a little salt, and the spirit would go find somewhere more hospitable to hang around.

This was different, though. Greta was being haunted by the ghost of her husband, and she could understand why. She was the one who left him buried on the edge of the Mississippi River in Rock Island County.

So apple pips and salt had done nothing. He continued to stand behind her in mirrors, move things she wanted to pick up while she was absently reaching for them, close doors that she was barely through, almost hitting her. Nonsense, really, but she knew that he would not rest until she put him to rest. Until she worked at making certain he was finally able to accept what had happened.

It was why she took the letters to the place where she had last seen him, both alive and dead. She drove the forty minutes to the city where they had parked, and had a bag with her that did not have a lunch or a book in it. Instead, she had a few oils, a trowel, and a packet of letters. Letters that she had been writing as the days waned and his figure remained standing in the reflection of her mirror even after she had finished brushing her teeth.

A chill wind brushed past her cheeks as Greta drove over the bridge, remembering that it was not nearly as cold the day she had been there with him. It was not the first time she was in the tree-laden riverbank across the Mississippi from Muscatine, but it was not a place she made a habit of going. Not because she was so distraught over her own actions, but because that river had its own ghosts, and while she could write letters to her husband, she could do nothing for the rest of them.

The first time Greta and her husband crossed that steel bridge from Iowa to Illinois, they stood together in the woodland of Rock Island County and watched the sun set. An autumn breeze pushed the collar of his jacket up against his unshaven chin and took pieces of her brown hair out of her simple ponytail while the sky was painted with a delicate brush of clouds. The second time they hiked down to the edge of the river, Greta left her husband there, buried beneath the loose soil under a pair of trees that had been twisted together during some great calamity decades ago. She had given him the water bottle filled with juice spiked with nightshade, and he had drained it without offering her even a mouthful, an action in due course of his normal behavior.

She waited then, letting him feel the tingling in his limbs that slowly stopped his movements. Something akin to regret touched her when he looked at her accusingly, his lips and tongue refusing to move well enough for him to make words. Eventually his heart and lungs stopped as well, and she got to work, burying him in a hole she slowly dug with a collapsible shovel in her pack. It only took her dumping the dirt over him to realize the regret was that she had waited so long to do something about him.

Now she returned to the place, relatively undisturbed, and relatively flat considering she had discarded some of the original dirt in other places to make room for him. She had made certain to bury him deep enough that wild animals would not be tempted by the scent of raw flesh. Greta could feel him there with her, a different ghost that was settled on the river than the others she knew had to be drifting around. The river was too full of history and the cycle of life and death to be anything but haunted. She imagined writing to all of them might put them all to rest, but she had no words for them.

No, her words were for the mound in front of her. Greta knelt down in the grass, making certain she was not about to kneel on some unseen creature hiding in the browning brush, and she pulled out her packet of letters. They were not in an envelope, and she had been very careful to write them on pages that were from a generic store tablet of paper. There was no reason to make things easier if someone wanted to come looking for him.

Untying the butcher's twine around the packet, she began to read the letters, though she read them out loud, as words seemed to escape the dead. Several of the pages were covered. A few had a single line on them. Others were a mishmash of drawings and words, not exactly sentences, but things that would mean something to them both. Greta used a loose rock to hold them down after reading each one.

"Dear Husband," she began, removing any power saying his name might have had there in that place of spirits.

"I imagine you're confused as to why a hike in the woods led to your death. The short answer is that you were too selfish to even bother to ask if I wanted a drink. Had you spared even a mouthful for me, you might still be alive. Unfortunately, you didn't give me any reason to want you around any longer. I suspect you might have figured out that I felt that way for a while.

"When I sat down to write to you, I can admit, I had a hard time putting this all into words. Perhaps I didn't want them to have any more power over me here than the actual emotions did at home. Maybe I just thought too many thoughts at once. I know that's one of the flaws you saw in me every time you looked my way. Anyway, I feel free. Finally."

Putting the paper down under the rock, she picked up another. "Dear Husband. There is nothing wrong with watching flowers sway in the breeze, or letting a rabbit nibble a flower bud or two. There is no reason to try and poison every single thing that doesn't fit your idea of a neat and tidy garden. It will take a long time for that to wash completely out of my herbs and carrots, but I'm willing to wait. Maybe you can appreciate it more, now that you're not going to worry about a perfect lawn."

Another note under the rock. She frowned at the next one, shaking her head. Those things were best left written, and she was certain she needed to keep that silent. Words had power. Words shaped the world around everyone and kept it moving. They reminded her of the river, the eternal rush of it in the back of the sounds that surrounded the area, coupled with the cacophony of traffic from the nearby bridge.

She put that to the side as well under the rock and picked up another letter. "Dear Husband. I suppose you are one of the ghosts of this place now. I have met some of the others, and I imagine you'll feel at home with them. Self-righteous indignation at being called out on your b.s. was your favorite emotion. They seem to feel the same way, these strange spirits. I suspect you'll find them irritating because they are as wrapped up in themselves as you are. That, by the way, is another reason you are where you are."

A few of the pages had scribbles on them, some dates, some just words. She remembered why December 23rd was on one of them. How he had asked her for a separation, then tried to pretend like they needed to celebrate the holidays first. As if it were some other gift to look forward to. He balked when she began packing a bag, realizing she was not going to stay and play house over the holidays to appease him, so he backpedaled and admitted he did not really want her to go.

Those pages went under the rock as well. When Greta had read all she could stand, all she could stomach, all she had had the mental fortitude to write out, she took the trowel out of her bag and dug a small hole over the ground where her husband was buried. She put the letters and the rock inside and buried them again. Lighting the candle, she poured the prepared oil over the site as well.

"It's time to say goodbye," she informed him. "It's . . . my time to say goodbye."

There was no acknowledgement that would have made a beautiful scene in a movie. No wind blew her hair, no rose dropped from out of nowhere. No bird twittered out of season and no voice trailed on the breeze with words of forgiveness. It was the parting of two people who no longer could love each other, and it was certainly not the bittersweet thing that fiction would have made out of it. She herself felt anger that could have only been described as long-coming, the end of a million painful encounters with someone who she had been foolish enough to give her heart to.

When Greta left the hidden burial site of her dead husband, she felt a lightness. That was all she would get when it came to the end of his time with her. It was enough, to write it out in those letters. It was enough to ease him into the story of the land, of a city she had barely ever visited, of a river that had existed longer than the spirits who clung to it. Even if she was the only one who knew the story.

Esperance Ciss

REJUVENATION

Eagle eyes scan the sky,
Feathers graze the clouds nearby.
My eyes follow as the bird soars.
Below, the Mississippi river contours,
Like tears and laughs map one's life.
A witness, my eyes adore.

My brain spins, again and again,
Raging in a whirling sea of flaws.
My hands long to touch, feel the world again!
My feet, ready to walk more miles,
May not run as fast, but miles they gain.

My skin sweating of new sensations,
Seeking the key to unlock jubilation.
Beats and rhythms, my heart begins
Lub-dup dances and life burns within.
My lungs gasping for new breaths,
Like ants searching for sugar on a pie.
New dreams rise, like sprouting tulips chase the sun.

Editor's note: WOTA has always welcomed new writers, and especially young writers. Sometimes we're lucky in that an entire talented family becomes part of WOTA, as word-loving parents cultivate word-loving kids. Such is the case with Kevin and Pearly. —M.U.

Photograph by Esperance Ciss

OH, FALL!

Crispy leaves rub my feet.
Red, yellow, brown, green.
Blustery wind sweeps my face.

Acorns everywhere,
Squirrels here and there,
Scamp the grass,
Climb the trees.

Oh! the birds,
Tweet, tweet, tweet!
In my mind,
I tumble into a
pile of leaves.
Fall is fun.
Fall is here!

Editor's note: Pearly wrote this poem at age 8, inspired by a walk with her mother through Weed Park. The accompanying photo shows the tree that inspired the poem. –M.U.

Kevin Ciss

INNOVATION

Robots made of brass,
And huge houses made of glass,
Automatic hover cars pass,
Through lush lawns filled with grass.

Plastic isn't trash,
Don't be so rash,
Old paper can be smashed,
So please reuse your trash.

What is future? I often wonder,
What is the past? I ask.
It is but a simple task,
Innovation,
Concentration,
And Jubilation.
We rise through the ages in tech,
But fall with shame.
Weapons and wonders,
This is the curse of life,
Till we die disgraced by our inventions.

Editor's note: Kevin Ciss' poem "Thanksgiving" placed first in the young writer's category of WOTA's 2018 poetry contest and is featured in the anthology *From River to River*. –M.U.

Dustin Joy

CHICORY

My calloused fingers find hers, smooth and soft. She smiles and swings our two hands back and forth extravagantly. We walk together feeling the heat in the soles of our shoes as the blacktop gives up a day's worth of sunshine. I take baby steps. She can't walk very far or very fast with her leg braces.

"What is that flower?" She pauses to allow a honeybee's evacuation and then bends at the waist until her nose touches the cornflower blue blossom at the side of the road. "It is sooooooo pretty."

"That's chicory." I sound it out for her and she forms the word, "chick-ree."

"It grows in the rocks. It's the bluest flower I ever saw. Isn't it pretty?"

"Yes, it is sweetheart."

She bends down again as if paying her respects to the chicory, an awkward curtsy. She sniffs. "Why does it grow in the rocks, and not in the garden with the other flowers?"

Our shadows lengthen, one long and one short. "The prettiest flowers grow in the rocks, my dear." Now she grips my fingers.

"Why, Daddy?"

"Nobody knows, my dear. Nobody knows why."

FATHER

It always passeth
my understanding
that God almighty,
who lit the stars
and dealt out planets
like a poker hand
and spun up the Milky Way
and summoned all of us
into existence
with a word,

needs,
nay, requires
nay, commands
our poor, pitiful praise,
our constant confirmation
of his glory,
our supplication
on bended knee,
our affirmation
of his
"mysterious ways."

Sending the tornado down one street,
giving neighbors a story to tell
on the other.
"Someone up there was looking out for us,
not so much for them."

Arbitrary punishments
for arbitrary crimes.
"Eat this fruit, not that fruit
or ... you'll die?"

"Don't look over your shoulder
at your friends
being brim-stoned
or ... you'll become
a pillar of salt?"

And then my wife and I
created a daughter
from an egg and a sperm
and some incantations.
I became
the almighty decider,
the payer of bills,
the layer down of laws
both sensible and
nonsensical,
and usually arbitrary.

"Eat thy broccoli,
lest thee be grounded."
"Steer clear of that boy."
"But why?"
"Because I sayeth so."

And, after awhile,
I find that,
as a minor deity,
I need,
nay, require
nay, command
the poor, pitiful praise
of our creation,
her constant confirmation
of my glory,
her supplication
on bended knee.
"Can I have the car keys, please?"

Her affirmation
of my
"mysterious ways,"
even as she rolls her eyes
to the heavens.

How cravenly
does a god
seek approval, affection, love
from his children.

SYCAMORE

There is a reason that mankind will never utterly do away with wild things, hard as we might consciously or unconsciously try to do so. The reason lies in the limited scope of man's perceptions and in the simple dogged persistence of nature.

There is little doubt that humans have the capacity, with bulldozers, end loaders, excavators, and trucks, to undo nature's patient workings of a thousand years. They have done it and they will continue to do it until the last trumpet blows. But they will not, ultimately, eradicate nature and natural things.

Along the Mississippi River, behind my father's house, grows a 100 foot tall sycamore tree. It is magnificent in its scale and bearing. I have stood at its base many times and looked up, slack-jawed, and just said *wow*!

How old it is I do not know. I could imagine its slow, relentless growth as Native Americans paddled by in dugout canoes. I could imagine Abe Lincoln stopping briefly at this pond to water his horse as he made his way to New Boston. I can picture generations of little boys growing up and growing old on this farm, fishing in this pond, helping their dads chop firewood in this forest, and ultimately chopping their own firewood and planting their own corn. The sycamore grew patiently next to the pond—a hundred years, two hundred, it is hard to know.

The sycamore, or one like it, will continue to grow behind my dad's house. As the generations of humans in this little town are born and live and go to their graves it will persist. It will grow patiently and each year it will scatter its little seed balls on the mud below. Someday, when the river is neither too high nor too low, one will put down roots in a forsaken spot no other plant has been able to exploit (for a thousand unknowable reasons) and it will begin to grow.

The generations of humans will live some more lives, and drive bulldozers even. It might be, after the sapling has pushed up six inches into the sky, that a careless hunter will visit the pond and step on it and push it down into the mud. It will be bent and may never recover its straight, proud bearing. But it will persist and start its crooked path toward the sun again. And perhaps, when it is six feet high, a buck deer will wander past with its velvety new antlers and rub some of the itchy stuff away on the little sycamore and in the process give it a deep wound that will be visible on its trunk for a hundred years.

Or perhaps the Corps of Engineers, in their wisdom, will determine that this little pond, good for nothing else, would be the perfect place to pump two cubic acres of sand dredged up from the bottom of the navigation channel. In that moment our little striving sapling will be buried alive and will perish. If the big tree still lives its environment will be so altered that it, too, will not recover. Or perhaps the Corps will simply cut it down to provide a road to their new sand pile. These local tragedies will only be a setback for nature, ultimately.

There have been so many such tragedies it would be impossible to catalog them. Maybe sycamores, altogether, will succumb to these thousand little insults and become extinct. In that day we will have hurt ourselves and we will have destroyed the sycamore family, but nature will simply move on. If you don't believe in the persistence of nature go to Hawaii and look at a volcano erupting and try to picture in your mind's eye how this devastation could turn into a verdant paradise brimming with life.

Even here, along the muddy Mississippi, some little cell of life will persist when the last sycamore is chopped into kindling. Maybe a cottonwood can tolerate the sand better. Maybe it will take the old sycamore's place and become the dominant life force in this vicinity. Maybe it won't be a tree. Maybe the deep sand will preclude any sapling from making another start here. Instead maybe the prickly pear that grows on the hills above will spread down into the new "desert" and use its special skills to translate a little sun and a little moisture into green paddles and pointy spikes.

Or maybe only some sort of algae or bacteria can make a beachhead here. But rest assured that it will grow, and given enough time, it will evolve, and maybe its generations, after millions of years, will make something like a sycamore again. And maybe not. Maybe it will evolve a sentient creature with dexterous hands and a big brain capable of building and driving a bulldozer.

Bill Nye has said "We do not need to save the world, we need to save the world for us." This is the point of conservation. The value of a sycamore tree, ultimately, is not to nature. Nature could not care less whether she exploits her resources with 100 foot sycamores or single celled algae. It is we, with the giant brains and the ability for aesthetic appreciation, who need a 100 foot sycamore if for no other reason than to look up, slack-jawed, and say *wow*.

IF THIS ISN'T NICE

Kurt Vonnegut, in his later years, concluded many of his speeches with a simple lesson. He was scrupulous about crediting the idea to his uncle Alex. He felt that a simple mental exercise had made his life better. In Vonnegut's words:

And I urge you to please notice when you are happy, and exclaim, or murmur, or think at some point, "If this isn't nice, I don't know what is."

I have been trying to take Vonnegut's advice to heart. I think his mantra contributes to a better life. I think it works in the present tense but, I would like to suggest, it applies quite as well to events in the past.

Memories are our possessions. More than any other kind of property they belong, personally, intimately, to us. Only dementia can steal away the treasure we possess in our memories. They can be called on for strength in times of trouble. They can be a reservoir of hope, and they can serve, per Vonnegut's suggestion, to uplift the spirit and remind the downtrodden that there once were good times and might be again.

Sometimes, when I am down or nursing a grievance, I go on a little mental journey. I am buoyed by a lovely memory, a piece of mental real estate which has been mine for nearly 40 years. It never fails to offer me comfort. I close my eyes and relive an afternoon from my childhood and, no matter the present circumstances, I feel better.

A boy of 14 and a man of 65 are in a boat. They are not speeding down the channel but floating, drifting among tall trees, the trunks of which have been overtaken by a spring flood. Here and there one can see little mounds of earth poking up through the floodwaters, but mostly it is a wet world. It is a wet world dappled with sunlight and filled with a the croaks of frogs, the plops of turtles, and the startled cries of wood ducks.

The boy guides the wooden boat with a pair of oars. He is a skinny boy with a notable awkwardness in his manner. He is no athlete and mostly lacks grace and coordination, that is, on land.

Here he is smooth and efficient, propelling the narrow craft between the maples and the cottonwoods quietly. He executes long power strokes when he can but is compelled, frequently, to retract one or the other oar into the boat, dripping, to avoid bumping a branch.

The boat is a beauty, his grandfather's pride, and the boy takes pride in it, too. He takes pride in its lovely alternating oak and pine ribs. He loves it for the sleek, elegant curve of its transom and the V shape of its bow. He loves the creaky brass oarlocks and the varnished gunwales. He loves this boat because he knows its history. He knows the story of how the boat was ordered from a catalog and arrived at the depot in town on the back of a railroad flatcar.

He can recite the outdoor sagas: this bow piled full of wild ducks and monster catfish whose length matched the boat's beam. The boy loves this boat precisely because it is an anachronism. It is an oddity among the fleets of metal jon boats which ply the Mississippi. Other fishermen have been known to mock it at the boat ramp as impractical. At this point in his life the boy sees the boat as a proxy. He is coming to realize that he himself is, if not an oddity, then at least odd. His quirky pastimes (collecting coins, reading the encyclopedia, flying model airplanes) are symptoms of a congenital "un-coolness" which will be made painfully manifest in high school.

There is a fine line between quirky and weird, after all, between eccentric and crazy. He senses this already. He knows that the lovely cheerleader who sits next to him in English class will not really be part of his life, his daydreams notwithstanding. If he has to be odd the boy wants, somehow, to be oddly beautiful, like his Grandpa's boat. That afternoon, enjoying nature, soaking in the sounds, the smells, the warmth, and taking in the wonderful curiosity of floating on an island, the boy is transported. He is transported from the daily life where he is an awkward, bumbling nerd to a place where he is competent and impressive and beloved.

I still have my grandpa's boat, and I am still odd. I retain the memory of that perfect day, and the flood, and the wood ducks, and my grandpa, sitting in the bow seat, leaning back and resting his head on a boat cushion. I still remember how the narrow sunbeams burrowed through the canopy of branches above and exploded in the rivulets of water running down the oars. I remember the serenity and the solitude and the perfection of the day.

Neuroscientists have demonstrated that the "use" of a memory, recalling it and then storing it away again, frequently alters or degrades it. Like the famous telephone game our memories undergo a loss of fidelity and can, in fact, begin to incorporate elements which were not present in the actual incident. But it may be that perfect fidelity is not what matters.

It may be that, as a crutch to mental health, a modified memory is just what the doctor ordered. My treasured afternoon with my grandpa is sweet to me and though it is possible that it did not occur as I describe it to you here, let alone how I might describe it to you in five years, or ten, it is of great value to my sanity. I miss my grandpa. I miss the way he cocked his head to listen for geese. I miss the rough feel of his five o'clock shadow when he would puff out his cheeks and I would run my little hand across the whiskers. I miss the way he would pretend to struggle with some simple mechanical device so that I could "help" him. And I miss the genuine and exuberant little whistle of appreciation he would give for some trifling achievement I had obtained. I have never had a greater cheerleader, and I never shall.

And so I draw on this memory frequently. I open the rusty file drawer and I pull out the yellowing folder. Inside is a photograph as vivid and as clear and as powerful as it was the day I put it there. I pull it out and I look at it and I remember. I think to myself, and I exclaim, or murmur (as is appropriate), "If this isn't nice, I don't know what is."

Dan Moore

EXPRESS YOURSELF

Our comfortable setting, with no bloodletting,
Is where freedom of expression
Welcomes each genre, happy to macabre,
Without a fear of rejection.

Here's chance to display, if you've something to say,
Whether by prompt or volition.
Just lay your soul naked, works you hold sacred,
In acts of humble submission.

You may dramatize, or perhaps mesmerize
Others with your cleverest craft.
Before a small crowd you will read yours aloud
And hope that you don't sound too daft.

They'll poke a big hole in the work of your soul,
Finding chances that you have missed
To build decent tension and, not to mention,
Failing to put heroes at risk.

These traditions, thirty years of submissions,
Of original written works,
Are our venue, Writers on the Avenue,
If a writer within you lurks.

WOTA ANNIVERSAY

It is not a cauldron; it's more like a bowl,
Where thoughts incomplete can come out whole,
To further be melded or become discarded,
Till expressions emerge full and wholehearted.

AND SO IT BEGAN

L arry strolls the avenue admiring the Christmas decorations put up courtesy of the Muscatine Chamber of Commerce. Needing his second cup of morning coffee, he pops into A Venue, a coffee shop and local favorite watering hole. The bell above the door announces his arrival and several patrons look to see who the newest arrival is.

"Hey, Larry, good morning," the shop owner says from behind the counter. "Coffee?"

"You read my mind, Helen. Is it fresh, or are you still repressing last night's coffee beans?"

She gives his hand a pat in mild rebuke as she places a mug in front of him and pours from her Bunn coffee pot. "Aren't you pleasant. You know it's fresh."

"I see the Christmas decorations are up. It seems Christmas starts earlier every year. Too much commercialization nowadays."

"That's progress for you," John, a Muscatine High School English teacher, says from three stools down at the counter.

"What progress? With the oil spill in Alaska and Reagan gone as president, I'm not sure what we have today is progress," Larry replies.

"Don't be such a pessimist, Larry," Helen chides him. "Get with the Christmas spirit. Bush may not be a bad president. He was ambassador to China and head of the CIA before becoming vice-president. How about the Berlin Wall coming down? Can't be all bad. Maybe we'll have some peace in the world for a change."

Larry takes another sip of his coffee. "That massacre in Tiananmen Square doesn't bode well in my book. I don't see world peace going anywhere. Can't turn on the news at night without seeing that the Soviets or the Red Chinese aren't doing something to breed hate and discontent. I hope 1990 is better than 1989 was."

The door jingles. Ginny enters carrying an oversized knitting bag with a partially completed something sticking out of the top with two protruding knitting needles.

111

"Hi, Ginny," sounds the counter chorus.

She waves hello in dismissal and takes up a seat at her usual table. "You got any of those iced cinnamon buns, Helen?"

"Of course I do; we always have them during the week. Want coffee with that?"

"Sure," Ginny says, removing her latest knitting project, a nondescript garment that has yet to take recognizable form. "I see they added new decorations to the street lamps for Christmas."

"We were just talking about that," says John.

"No we weren't," retorts Larry. "We were discussing how bad the evening news is. There's nothing good on television anymore."

His statement draws the attention of Susan, a housewife who drops by A Venue twice a week to read her newspaper and enjoy coffee. "You need to change channels, John. 'Family Matters' and 'Coach' are pretty funny."

"Yeah, I saw them last week. They were a hoot," Helen says, delivering Susan's coffee and a dinner plate-sized pastry. "Anything interesting in the paper, Susan?"

"The comics. Here, I finished them at home, but I'm still reading the rest."

"You sure?" The owner folds the section of newsprint under her arm.

"Take it, I'm done. I can't read the paper at home anymore. The kids are all gone, either working in Des Moines or off to college, and Ted's at work over at HON. It gets lonely around the house now. So I come here just to see another human being."

"Gee, thanks," Larry says. "I'm glad to be good for something, even if it's just as a backdrop for your sanity."

"Sorry, I didn't mean it that way. We have some good discussions here. You all keep my light on the world lit. I do appreciate you."

John clinked his spoon on the side of his cup as if to say "Here, here."

"The news can get you down," Larry says. "The stuff on TV is mindless; it's not challenging, no matter how much I watch. They haven't even come out with any good movies lately."

"How about that one about baseball, *Field of Dreams*? That was pretty good," Helen says, back behind her spot at the counter.

"Haven't seen it," says John.

"It's what I call a 'feel good' movie," Helen adds.

"I'll grant you that it was good," agrees Bob, another regular sitting at a back table who has come over to join the conversation. "I do have to say, however, on the whole, movies and TV are just as Newton Minnow described them a few years ago. They're a 'vast wasteland'. Have you seen *Baywatch*?"

"Wouldn't miss it," Larry grinned, drawing looks from the women.

"It was a rhetorical comment, Larry. I don't think writers know how to write anymore. They turn out vapid works that do nothing to engage our minds. And ever since Danielle Steele started pumping out her stuff onto the best sellers list, books aren't doing that much better. I can probably write something better than what's out there now given half a mind, a typewriter, and a little time."

"Why don't you do it, Bob. You're retired. What have you got to do with your time, now?" Larry's comment was more supportive than sarcastic.

"That doesn't sound like such a bad idea," Susan says. "I bet all of us could write something if we put our minds to it."

"What do we know about writing?" John motions to Helen for a refill. "It's harder than you think. I teach English to your kids, and let me tell you, it's hard enough just to get them to write a simple subject and a predicate. What are we? Just a group of retirees, housewives, and shop owners."

"But we have life's experience to fall back on," Ginny says, wiping a wayward crumb and glob of icing from her chin. "I think Bob's right. What *have* we got to lose? I liked English classes in high school and college. I was never good at them, but I appreciate a good story when I can find one. We should try it."

Five sets of eyes stare at her to see if she is putting them on.

"Hey, I'm serious. What do we have to lose — an afternoon or evening wasting time in front of the boob tube? How hard can it be? It would be more interesting than watching them celebrate a touchdown or critique some rock concert."

"Okay, say we do it," Bob says. "Where would we go?"

"All we'd need is a few chairs, some decent lighting, and a few tables. We've got pen and paper and our minds. We should exercise them for a change," Ginny says.

They are at a momentary impasse until Helen says, "We could meet here at A Venue. I've got a private dining room in the back. We don't have much call for private dinners anymore. It's not as if I'm putting the space to good use now."

The six looked at each other, waiting for someone to refute or take up the dare.

Finally, Ginny takes up the challenge. "Okay, I'll start. Let's pick a night."

"Why not? Susan says. "Ted can fend for his own dinner one night a month."

"Bring him along," Helen offers. "I could make a stew or barbeque, some kind of comfort food for the spouses, while you guys dip into your inkwells and scratch with your quills."

John is intrigued by the idea. "A once a month getaway might not be such a bad idea. But if we do it, what will we call our group?"

"We have to have a name?" Larry asks.

"Yes," Ginny and Susan say at the same time.

"Well, Autocrat of the Breakfast Table and Algonquin Round Table are already taken," John says. "How about Night Writers in Muscatine?"

Five heads shake at his suggestion.

Then Helen offers, "How about Writers at A Venue?"

"Hmm, it has possibilities," Ginny says.

"But it doesn't quite flow," John says. "I got it. How about Writers on the Avenue? Get it?"

Bill Telle

CARPE UNUM

One day
One hour
One minute
One second
One thought
One misstep
One movement
One mistake
One pause
One I love you
One breath
One heartbeat
Separates us
From now and then
From life and death.
Cherish now
Everyone
And every one.

Author's note: This was written in response to a writing prompt for the September 2019 meeting to write something that borrows from or works like a round (rondo/rondeau). –B.T.

NOWHERE LOVE

I drift into sleep
with promises to keep
and secrets to know
You ignite my dreams
and it always seems
love has nowhere to go

I hold you tight
as the endless night
keeps our love at bay
But as night rolls on
past the endless dawn
love has nowhere to stay

I ask if you'll remain
to ease the pain
of emptiness inside
You say you'll stay
until the break of day
when love has nowhere to hide

I speak your name
as the endless game
is shared by you and me
The cards are played
from the deck we made
when love had nowhere to be

I drift awake
with promises to break
and endless secrets to know
You retreat from my dreams
and it always seems
love has nowhere to go

Jodie Toohey

THE FIRE OF CREATING

Like the log in
My backyard copper fire pit,
I burn
From the inside out.
Worms of molten fire
Cut their way,
Meandering through
The dried oak flesh,
Burrowing tunnels
Until flame bursts out,
White-hot, blue, then dancing orange.
I spit and crackle truth,
Shards of lit-up ash
Flits into cool indigo air,
Then distinguished, smoky grey,
Exhausted, floats back.
After my energetic creation,
Sometimes violent,
Sometimes subdued, comfortable
Passing minutes in seconds,
I relax into embers
Rolling like a mound of snakes
Curling over each other
Until no more, energy depleted
Just carbon and ash
Waiting to be cleaned out
For the next Saturday night fire.

CIRCULATION

You flip my pages
In a frantic effort.
Can't wait to use me,
Abuse me,
And throw me back.
Your sticky, rough,
And dirt-crusted fingers —
Sometimes crumple me,
Sometimes can barely stand
To run their tips
Along my edges,
Making that horribly
Irritating, scratching
That sends ripples
Up my perfect-bound spine.
Coffee rings, sneezes,
All thrust upon me
And collect in
Crevices between my pages.
Some devour me,
Some a mere "eh,"
And toss me to the take-back pile.
Some don't even take me –
Just flip my pages
And return me to the wrong order
So no one can ever find me again.
Dogs and children have
Chewed me.
And I've seen more
From perches on bedside tables
Than anything ever should.
But at least I'm not on some
Used book card table sale
Waiting to be sentenced
To the I'll-read-it-when
I've-read-everything-else pile.
I'm still in circulation.

Misty Urban

Editor's note: This was a response to the May 2017 word challenge for which the given words were anthology, heirloom, esoteric, whimsical, crewel, jubilee, mystify. See Bob Bancks's animal fable on p. 85 for another example. –M.U.

JUBILEE

My mother rests her elbows on the lip of a box and puts her head in her hands. "What a pile of — of . . . stuff." I'm 34 years old and she still can't swear in front of me.

I look over the stack of boxes and tubs and albums and file folders, the unfinished anthology of my grandmother's life. The piles of *Reader's Digest*. The watch inscribed with the name of my great-uncle who died before I was born. Scarves and sweaters and those obnoxiously patterned shirts with the deep front pockets that could hold her Kleenex, her room keys, and a paperback book.

"There's not all that much here, when you think about it. She could have left us something old and valuable, like an heirloom. Or a magic lamp. This stuff is just . . . what do you say? Esoteric?" I reach for the word, but it floats beyond me, veiled. I know the meaning I want to capture, but not the words to frame it. Like this strange and fleeting glimpse into my grandmother's left-behind life.

My mother fiddles with the lid of another cardboard box. "Eclectic." I can see her lips tighten. She's trying to be all smiles around me lately, brave and stiff-upper lip, but every time she glances my way, she looks at my chin. Not at the scarf covering my head, and not the scar beneath it. "Or maybe whimsical?"

I put my hand on the pile of scarves and move them toward me. Grandma had gotten cantankerous in her old age, a real shrew, but these scarves are pieces of art.

"Not this. What is it? I'm mystified." It isn't the word I wanted, but it works. So many things now are these near misses. This touching near a place I knew.

119

"That's crewel. There was some class she was taking."

"Cruel is right. It looks like a deranged caterpillar."

"Oh, *Suzy* . . ." Her lips twitch, but she isn't laughing. She bites down hard on her lower lip, the thing she does to keep from crying. My mother has been so brave for so long. First my father, then her eldest daughter running away to find herself in the Philippines and finding a boy instead. Losing her mother to dementia and demons, and now me, the daughter who was supposed to be the support of her old age, with a brain tumor that is growing back. Nothing about this is what she was promised.

"Let's have a jubilee," I say.

Her eyes get that sad, cloudy look that tell me I'm making word salad again. "Do you mean junk auction?"

"No." I draw a scarf off the top of the pile. It explodes with flowers, fireworks of flowers, bouquets of flowers. I would do anything to erase that bewilderment in my mother's eyes. I drape the scarf over her beautiful silver-white hair. I can't ease her heart over her mother's death. I can't tell her how scared I am. But I can pretend, as she's doing, that everything will be fine. That I found exactly the word I wanted.

"I mean a big old party," I say. "A diamond jubilee, like the Queen has. Grandma was the queen. And now you are."

She looks at me for a moment. Then she reaches up and ties the scarf at her hairline, just like the knot in mine. Her mother taught me this. We are a line of fierce and burdened women, draping our scars and our hurts with the colors of defiance.

"And you will be queen after me?" she asks. She reaches over the boxes and grips my hands.

"I will," I promise. And at last, she smiles.

Editor's note: This is another take on the word challenge for January 2018 with the words bouquet, joy, happiness, stupefy, nightmare, resolution, begin, handy, gout, grovel, and splendiferous. See Judy's piece on page 49. –M.U.

FIRST DAY JITTERS

"Here, try this," my brother said, handing me a splendiferous bouquet. The flowers were about three feet tall and looked big enough to eat a person.

"Well, that's handy," I said, taking the vase. "I was wondering how to apologize." The glass was heavy. "Didn't you buy these for Rosie?"

"Let's talk about *your* nightmare," he said. "I can't believe you hit your professor on the first day of class."

"Stupefying, I know," I admitted. I wanted him to say more about Rosie, but he'd never appreciated my prying. I'd made a resolution to keep my mouth shut. Their happiness seemed claustrophobic from the beginning, too much too soon, but it didn't make me feel vindicated to know I'd been right.

"Well, I suppose I should commence with the groveling," I said. "I don't suppose I'll get an A now?"

"How bad was it?" my brother asked. "Snapped femur? Gouts of blood?"

"A bruised hip, I think. He's under observation."

"I'll go order him a good painkiller." My brother stood, patted the pencil in the pocket of his white coat. "You all right?"

"I hit my literature professor in the parking lot," I told him, struggling to my feet with the vase. "The semester could have started better. Are *you* all right?"

He shrugged and didn't look at me. "Fine," he said. "I'm always fine. Everything's fine here."

With the enormous bouquet of flowers in my arms, I couldn't even hug him. He was the older brother, the competent physician, and I was the screw-up he had to bail out again. I watched him walk through the clinic, all the nurses and therapists casting him smiles, and I wished Rosie were around so I could dump the flowers on her head. Still, I knew this was my fault. So used to taking care of me, he'd married a woman he had to put back together, and now she had gone and broken his heart.

Author's note: This was written to rise to the October 2017 challenge to use the words hirsute, defenestrate, prevaricate, supercilious, anarchy, odiferous, contempt, discombobulated, and geothermal. The more outrageous the words, the more fun it is writing the piece. –M.U.

BLIND DATE

The date went wrong the moment I stepped in his car.

"Don't touch anything," he said. "I just Armor-alled the seats."

That explained the overwhelming smell. Between the wafts of Polo coming at me and the odiferous upholstery, I was going to be discombobulated before we got to the restaurant, and not for the reasons he wanted.

"Sons of Anarchy," he said, plugging in his iPod, and turned the music up too loud.

I'll show you anarchy, I thought. I was only doing this as a favor for a friend. He clearly thought he was doing me the service, gifting me with his company.

At the stoplight, he poured contempt on the other drivers. "Green arrow, grandma. Can't you see over the wheel? Get a move on, dipwad. I gotta show this lady a good time."

He pulled a black comb out of his pocket and scraped it over his coiffure. I had never met a more supercilious or hirsute man. But what could I do? Defenestrate myself? I'd get squashed in the intersection.

I'll say this for me: I don't prevaricate. I just flat-out lie. When the Applebee's hostess palmed the menus and inquired, "Two?" I said, "Nope, we're not together. I've never seen this guy in my life."

I went straight to a bar table, ordered a Dollarita, and called my best friend.

"Fifteen minutes," I reported. "I didn't survive the car ride."

When she showed up we ordered more Dollaritas, followed by spinach queso, and as we do on everything else, we agreed: just because a man works for a geothermal installer doesn't mean he has any depth.

Author's note: This was written in response to a challenge brought by WOTA member Anna Counter to begin a piece with these lines: "She rocked. In a little while the faint, damp, muddy river smell would come drifting up on the fog." As usual, I didn't quite follow the instructions; I put the lines at the end. The piece was later published in the online journal *Fiction Attic*. –M.U.

RIVER BOTTOM

She sat on the deep wooden porch in the chair her grandfather had made, and she rocked. The evening clouds, dark in their underbellies, clumped and hurried toward the line of beech trees lining the creek. The insects hummed and the birds chittered and the frogs croaked nervously, and once in a while the big garrulous *ga-THUMP* of the bullfrog belched through the other noise.

From the bedroom inside the house she heard the same sporadic hacking, the guttural expulsion and then the dry wretched scratching for air. Behind it was the rattle she'd heard before, when the grandfather who'd shaped this chair had lain, years ago, in that very bed, choking up lungs tarred black by a life in the coal mines. When she heard that rattle, she came out on the porch to wait.

No one worked in the coal mines anymore; now they blew up mountains and scraped the top flat as an angel cake, pushed the blasted rubble and the twisted roots of the great oaks and spruces into the valleys, suffocating rivers, towns, a whole way of life. Fast, maybe. But not clean. Death never was.

Some time ago, before the belly of the sun had reached the far blue hill, he'd stopped calling her name, ceased the faint, desperate cackle for "Ell – Ell—Ell." Soon it would all cease, all of it. The spitting up of his saliva and the stomach lining poisoned by lead, nicotine, the many strange compounds with their haunting names that he had breathed by choice and by lack of choice all his life. The querulous "Nell! Get in here, you good-for-nothin!" The curses, the hand flat and hot against her rear or the back of her head, or pointed, as it had once or twice, toward the shotgun leaning behind the door. The hands that had been so eager and fumbling in their cold softness on her wedding night, when she was bought and unwrapped like a slab of meat. All the times that heavy imprint had come with a "Dammit, it's for your own good!" or "Why you make me do these things?" or "Wipe that look off your face, or you'll get it agin." You could hardly blame a man for doing what he'd seen other men do all his life, for doing what he was driven to do. But you could hardly blame a woman, could you, if the bruises went deep and lodged there, waiting.

She wasn't unchristian; she'd left a glass of water by the bed. He couldn't reach it. It wouldn't help. Tomorrow she would look on a new sunrise, a new land, the land that had belonged to her family for a hundred years and would now belong only to her, the fields, the creek bottom, the ancient trees that had not yet been gutted by disease or rot or bulldozers dowsing for coal. She listened to the dry scratching voice and the way it blended with the frogs, like a chorus of nature, no sentient thought behind it but the desperate wish to survive. She listened to the bullfrog bellow and stop. She rocked. In a little while the faint, damp, muddy river smell would come drifting up on the fog.

Clio Vogel

AUTUMN LEAVES

leaves

crunchy   flat

falling   blowing   changing

color   full

display

Editor's note: Clio won second place in the young writer's division of WOTA's 2018 poetry contest and her series of diamante poems were published in *From River to River*. This poem, written as a continuation of that series, was composed when she was 7 and performed at WOTA's 2018 holiday party and open mic. –M.U.

Young writer Clio Vogel performing
at the WOTA holiday party and open mic
Photo by Misty Urban

Rebecca Whitmore

SILENT SCREAMS

He was so little interested — just as when people speak of the weather — that he did not notice whether I made him any answer or not. He didn't expect one.

He rambled on about his plans to finally visit Italy. All the sites he would see. He knew I always wanted to visit there, with him. Now he was going. He didn't say he wished I could go too.

His phone vibrated. A text he didn't try to hide. I could make out some of the words — something about a river cruise and his favorite bottle of wine. I wanted to ask about his plans, but he didn't expect me to.

I noticed his wedding ring was missing. There wasn't a tan line. How long since he'd worn it?

Another text. He smiled as he read it. That sexy chuckle from deep within, something I hadn't heard in a long time.

He slowly stood, finally looking at me, that rare moment of his focus on me — my eyes, my face, my body. Sadness appeared in his eyes, but with a blink, it passed. The knock at the door had his attention now.

Come in. Yes, I'm about to leave. In fact, I'll be going out of the country. No, I don't know when I'll be back.

The nurse rearranged my pillow and asked how I was feeling today — just as when people speak of the weather — that she did not notice whether I made her any answer or not. She didn't expect one.

I'm in here! I've always wanted to go to Italy! You promised me!

Silent screams left me feeling more trapped than my lifeless body had ever made me feel.

I wish I had died. I know he did too.

Image by Rebecca Whitmore

A fairy godmother passed this way
or so I want to believe.
Leaving a sign just for me
on this day too heavy to breathe.

The tiptoed girl approached, removing
the earring from the branch,
hypnotized by the magic of dew
and crystal touched by sunlight.
The spell broken, she looks my way
offering a view of her treasure
and asking if it is mine.

CONTRIBUTOR'S NOTES

Robin Abbott is relatively new to Iowa, having moved here in 2018. Through a genetic deformity, she was born completely without imagination, thus she has written a non-fiction book about her work in pediatric occupational therapy. With WOTA's help, she is learning to use her intellect as a substitute for creativity, as a person born without arms learns to use their feet with prehensility. She is grateful to have found WOTA.

Patricia Regan Argiro's poem "Advisement" first appeared in the 2000 WOTA anthology.

Alan Arkema was born in Iowa, though he spent his career as a clergyman in various states, as well as five years in Australia. His hobbies include writing short stories and novels for his own enjoyment, though he often sends pieces to family members and friends. WOTA holds a special place in his writing life. The monthly word challenges present an opportunity for him to at times engage his 'silly side,' i.e. the word challenge included in this anthology.

Bob Bancks started writing after retiring from farming. His stories vary from children's animal tales to romantic novels. He credits the inspiration for his animal tales to the many years he and his lovely wife Jane raised pigs and sheep and encountered many of the woodland animals who ventured into their buildings. He hopes you enjoy reading his musings as much as he does writing them.

Mike Bayles, a lifelong Midwest resident, writes about human connections with nature, settings (mostly rural), and with each other. He writes fiction, poetry, mixed genre pieces, and the occasional essay. His work *Breakfast at the Good Hope Home,* a literary collage, tells a story about a son visiting his Alzheimer's father in the nursing home. He appreciates the support and fun activities that Writers on the Avenue has offered.

Jeff Boldt (1954-2019) was a good storyteller. His imagination was a gift he discovered early in life and he sometimes drew inspiration from the most unlikely places. It was a gift he gladly shared with the young and the young at heart through his toy stores, A Planet's Wild and Teddy and Friends; his self-published books; and his writings and contributions as a member of Writers on the Avenue. To read more about Jeff and his work, visit http://www.boldtworks.com.

Judy Chapman was raised in Muscatine and lived in California for 25 years before returning. She runs a piano studio from her home. She began writing as a journalist and for the last 20 years has switched to prose and essays. She joined Writers on the Avenue in 1993.

Kathy Geren Christy is a lifelong reader and writer, belonging to as many as five book groups at a time. As a member of The Society of Great River Poets, she has enjoyed the feedback and suggestions of WOTA member Pat Bieber. Something she particularly enjoys when reading both literature and poetry is the great range of style and voice of authors and poets.

Esperance "Hope" Ciss likes to step outside her comfort zone and explore other literary genres. Currently, she is working on her memoir, *The Glass is Half Empty*. The knowledge, passion and dedication of WOTA members have been the driving energy for her inspiration. She also contributed to the 2018 anthology *From River to River*. When she is not writing, she likes to volunteer her time and skills in making a difference in the lives of people everywhere. To learn more about Esperance and her work, visit her website, invisionhope.com.

Kevin Ciss's writing life began with his English teacher's acknowledgment of his descriptive and analytical abilities. He enjoys reading, writing, and telling stories. His poem "Thanksgiving" appears in the 2018 WOTA anthology, *From River to River*. Kevin is a middle school student who enjoys sharpening his wrestling skills as well as learning new jargon like farming points, suplex, stalling, gassed, and more, which sounds like a word challenge list for his next writing project.

Pearly Ciss is a happy 8-year-old who loves spending time outdoors. The poem "Oh, Fall!" captures her curiosity and excitement in nature. Occasionally, Pearly enjoys a treat when she visits WOTA meetings.

David R. Collins was an accomplished writing teacher, widely published author, and a pillar of the Quad Cities writing community who founded the Midwest Writing Center in 1980 and launched the Mississippi Valley Poetry Contest, Children's Literature Festival, and Mississippi Valley Writers Conference. "Sunset" appeared in the first WOTA anthology published in 1991.

Dave Cooney is a frequent contributor to WOTA when he is not riding RAGBRAI, tending the Muscatine Arboretum, planting pollinator gardens, and helping out the Muscatine community in other significant ways.

Anna Counter is the author of *I'm Jesse* and *Two Paths, One Understanding*. She notes: As a writer I have gained so much from so many places. First is my deep desire to write. Second is the insight and help that I received from Writers on the Avenue, and last through watching and listening to the world and the people around me. Thanks to all.

Aldeen Davis was an active early member of Writers on the Avenue in addition to her deep community involvement on the city and state levels. She wrote a long-running column, "Soul Food for Thought" in the *Muscatine Journal*, which she later turned into a book. "Ebony Moth" appeared in the 1992 WOTA anthology and "Pipe Dream" in the 2000 anthology.

Duffy De France dreamed up WOTA in 1989 and the first official meeting of Writers on the Avenue was held in February 1990. She has since remained active in the regional arts scene, with roles in the Bi-State Literary board and the Muscatine County Arts Council. Duffy began the Sidewalk Poetry contest which has resulted in multiple WOTA members having their poems printed in concrete around Muscatine, including an exquisite corpse poem by several WOTA members honored in the inaugural contest.

Kimberly Dickens graduated from Muscatine High School, served active duty in the Air Force, and earned a bachelor's degree in English from the University of Iowa. She is past president of WOTA. Poetry is her first love, but she is also a science fiction enthusiast, essayist, painter, and gamer. Her poem "Lost Power" first appeared in the 2010 WOTA anthology and "Modern Alchemy" in the 2011 edition.

Barbara Dockery's poem "Humility" appeared in the premier WOTA anthology (1991).

Lucile Adkins Eye's poem "When I Am Old" appeared in the 1995 WOTA anthology.

Mike Fladlien is a retired business education teacher. His passions are economics, drawing, and writing haiku. He has been published in several WOTA anthologies, including *From River to River*.

Monica Flink is an award-winning author and baker who has been writing for over twenty-five years, occasionally with the assistance of her very helpful cat, Cinder. She currently works in the Quad Cities area as a graphic designer and would like to thank Writers on the Avenue for their support of writers and the literary arts in the area. Without WOTA, many voices would remain unheard and stories would remain unread. Her work is dedicated to her first and biggest fan: her mother.

Judy Haskins has lived in the Muscatine area most of her life. Her short stories reflect her love of family and nature. She also enjoys writing, painting and gardening. She is thankful to the Writers on the Avenue for the friendship, free workshops, supportive critiquing, and the opportunity to learn about and try new things.

Katherine E. "Kitty" Jones was a founding member of WOTA. Her poem "Someday When Old" appeared in the 1995 anthology.

Dustin Joy is an airline pilot and writer who lives in western Illinois with his wife and three children. He enjoys fishing, gardening, and beekeeping, none of which he's very good at. He writes for *Plane and Pilot Magazine*, has been published at http://www.naturewriting.com and http://femmeliterate.net, and blogs at http://stuffiminterestedin.com. He has been a WOTA member since 2017.

Ron Lackey is a life-long resident of the Muscatine area. He is attending the University of Arizona to attain his Master's degree in English studies with the intent of teaching English in Montana.

Mary Kay Lane's Barbie poem appeared in the 1996 anthology and her poem "Since You Didn't Ask, I'll Tell You About the Pelicans Anyway" won first place in the adult division of WOTA's 2016 poetry contest. She lives in Canton, Missouri where she works part-time at the public library. While frequently inspired, she admits she does not write poems as often as she should.

Jason Liegois has been a resident of eastern Iowa and Muscatine for more than 30 years. His interest in writing was sparked as a teenager, which led him into careers as a newspaper reporter and educator. He started participating regularly in WOTA when he moved back to Muscatine in 2007, which encouraged him to return to fiction writing and experiment with poetry. His debut novel *The Holy Fool* was published in 2019.

Nadine Lord was an extensively published author and a frequent contributor to WOTA. Her Emily Dickinson poem first appeared in the 1996 anthology.

Tomma Lous Maas's poem "Earth Metals" appeared in the 1995 WOTA anthology.

Ralph Montrone lives in Burlington, IA, and is a member of the Society of Great River Poets.

Dan Moore graduated from Duke University and served 27 years as a submarine officer in the U.S. Navy, retiring with the rank of Captain. He has published in the *Naval War College Review* and *The River Cities Reader*. He has earned prizes for fiction in the Midwest Writing Center's annual Iron Pen contest, has poems appearing in

WOTA's 2018 anthology *From River to River* and in the 2019 *Lyrical Iowa*, and has been featured on the literary radio show "Scribbles" on WVIK 90.3 FM.

Betty Mowery was active in WOTA and her poem "The Dancer" first appeared in the 1996 anthology. She lives in Rock Island, IL.

Gesene Oak is a long-time member of Writers on the Avenue. She enjoys writing poetry to avoid working on her novel. Other writing groups she belongs to include The Society of Great River Poets, Midwest Writing Center, and University Writing Club. She has also been a member of the Iowa Poetry Association for many years and has had her poems selected for inclusion in IPA's anthology, *Lyrical Iowa*, for nineteen successive years. WOTA members know her as **Pat Bieber.**

Kit Redeker is another Muscatine citizen who was active on the literary scene. Her poem "The Towers" first appeared in the 1996 WOTA anthology.

A graphic artist and cartoonist, **Daniel Roberts'** artwork has appeared in magazines and publications as well as a continuing comic strip named "Haley's Comment" that appears in the newspaper *Toons*. He has written and illustrated four cartoon books, a number of children's picture books including the Harrison and his Dinosaur Robot series and *There's a Cookie Stuck to my Nose*, easy-reader chapter books including *Boy and Dinosaur, The Two Witches* and *Douglas Diggly Super Spy,* and the Pep Squad Mysteries series for young readers. His cartoons have appeared in the Writers on the Avenue anthologies since 2017.

Sharon Savage and her husband, Tom, were both members of WOTA, which met for a while at their bookstore, Muscatine Books and More. Sharon wrote the "Dispatches from Downtown" column for the *Muscatine Journal* and her "Holloween" poem, which first appeared there, was also printed in the 2006 WOTA anthology.

Betty Smith was a long-time WOTA member and her work appeared in many WOTA anthologies. "Marriage Quilt" first appeared in the 2005 edition.

Denise Smith lives in Nichols, Iowa. Her father instilled a love of reading in her at an early age. Nature is a wonderful teacher and is reflected in her writing. She was a member of WOTA for 18 years and truly enjoys the camaraderie and support from the members.

Dick Stahl was a beloved English teacher, the Quad Cities' first poet laureate, and the author of four books of poetry. He was featured in WOTA's premier anthology and his poem "Red Paint Sale" appeared in the 1996 edition. Dick passed away shortly before this anthology went to print, and he will be deeply missed.

Bill Telle is a self-unemployed Muscatine resident of 46 years. He writes poetry and song lyrics in his spare time. In his unspare time he rides his bicycle and plays the saxophone, not simultaneously.

Dan Titus was born in Wilton, Iowa, and lived most of his life in Muscatine. He was a member of Writers on the Avenue for nearly 30 years. He writes goofy poetry and short humorous stories of the tall tale variety.

Jodie Toohey is the author of nine books: three poetry collections: *Crush and Other Love Poems for Girls* (2008), *The Other Side of Crazy* (918studio, 2013), and *Versed in Nature: Hiking Northwest Illinois and East Iowa State Parks* (2017); five novels: *Missing Emily: Croatian Life Letters* (2012), *Melody Madson – May It Please the Court?* (2014), *Taming the Twisted* (2015), *Taming the Twisted 2: Reconstructing Rain* (2018), and *Shattered Pearl* (2019); and one nonfiction book, *Book Marketing Basics: The 5 Ps*. When she is not writing fiction or poetry, Jodie helps authors, soon-to-be authors, and want-to-be authors from pre-idea to reader through her Wordsy Woman Author Services company. She's also helping individuals to tell their story through her publishing company, Legacy Book Press.

Misty Urban joined WOTA in 2015, shortly after moving to Muscatine. She credits WOTA members with helping her polish several pieces for publication and for being the reason she received an Outstanding Literary Arts Educator Award from the Midwest Writing Center. She has served as vice-president, president, and secretary/treasurer for WOTA and has enjoyed every minute. You can find more about her publications at mistyurban.net.

Clio Vogel placed in WOTA's 2018 poetry contest and since then has gone on to write many more poems and stories, often accompanied with original artwork. Currently a third grader, she loves roller blading, playing soccer, reading, and learning Spanish. She wants to be an airplane pilot when she grows up.

Rebecca Whitmore has always enjoyed creating—poetry, short stories, inukshuks, mixed media art, and books for her grandchildren. A regular contributor to *Lyrical Iowa* and WOTA publications, she takes pride in her poem etched in a downtown sidewalk...until the upcoming revitalization project. She wrote *Boots: At Home at MCSA*, given to children that stay at the homeless shelter, and *Find A Penny*, a children's book written for the Community Foundation of Greater Muscatine.

OTHER BOOKS BY WOTA

Winter Holidays in the City of Pearls

Climbing the Hill of Life:
Stories and Art to Inspire and Uplift

From River to River:
Thoughts on Life in the Great Bend

ABOUT WRITERS ON THE AVENUE

Writers on the Avenue is a non-profit literary organization dedicated to promoting the literary arts in and around Muscatine, Iowa. WOTA has been supporting local authors since 1990.

Find out more about events, activities, and publications by visiting
http://writersontheavenue.wordpress.com

Made in the USA
Monee, IL
07 June 2020